Grammar and Punctuation

Grammar 1 Teacher's Guide

Carol Matchett

Schofield & Sims

Free downloads available from the Schofield & Sims website

A selection of free downloads is available from the Schofield & Sims website (www.schofieldandsims.co.uk/free-downloads). These may be used to further enhance the effectiveness of the programme. The downloads add to the range of print materials supplied in the teacher's guides. They include the following items:

- a **Curriculum coverage chart**
- an enlarged **Focus text** for each lesson
- a **Dictation assessment sheet**
- a **Pupil target reminder**
- a **Learning pathways class chart** for each year group
- a **Final test analysis class chart** for each year group.

Published by **Schofield & Sims Ltd**, Dogley Mill, Fenay Bridge, Huddersfield HD8 0NQ, UK
Telephone 01484 607080
www.schofieldandsims.co.uk

This edition copyright © Schofield & Sims Ltd, 2017
First published in 2017

Author: **Carol Matchett**
Carol Matchett has asserted her moral rights under the Copyright, Designs and Patents Act, 1988, to be identified as the author of this work.

British Library Cataloguing in Publication Data
A catalogue record for this book is available from the British Library.

Design by **Oxford Designers & Illustrators Ltd**

Printed in the UK by **Page Bros (Norwich) Ltd**

ISBN 978 0 7217 1391 5

Contents

Introduction

Schofield & Sims Grammar and Punctuation is a structured whole-school scheme for teaching grammar and punctuation while also building on vocabulary, reading and writing skills. It can be used alongside the **Schofield & Sims Spelling** series for complete Spelling, Punctuation and Grammar [SPaG] coverage.

Grammar and Punctuation is designed to progressively develop knowledge and understanding of grammatical concepts through six teacher's guides and six pupil books containing a carefully structured sequence of lessons. The teacher's guides provide you, the teacher or adult helper, with notes and activities to support the teaching of these lessons, annotated answers to the pupil book questions, and a variety of assessment resources for tracking progress.

Supporting a mastery approach, the focus of this programme is on rich practice, deep and secure understanding and fluency in application. The pupils not only learn the terminology and correct usage of grammar and punctuation, but they also build up the skills, knowledge and confidence to apply them in their own independent writing. All pupils are encouraged to move at the same pace through the lessons and are given the same opportunity to fully understand the concept being taught. A wealth of practice questions, writing tasks, activity ideas and resources are provided to support the wider application of the grammar and punctuation that has been learnt in each lesson and to help the pupils to truly master the art of writing.

The programme is designed primarily for pupils in Years 1 to 6, and the concepts and terminology that are introduced are in line with the National Curriculum for English. However, understanding of grammar and punctuation is cumulative, so grammatical terms and concepts introduced in one book are revisited and developed further in subsequent books to reinforce the pupils' understanding. In particular, concepts and areas of learning introduced towards the end of one book are revisited and embedded in the next book to further ensure consolidation and continuity.

There are 15 corresponding lessons in **Grammar 1** and its related **Teacher's Guide**, five for each term. These lessons follow the statutory requirements for Year 1 'Vocabulary, grammar and punctuation' in the National Curriculum for English, including Appendix 2, while also promoting and supporting other aspects of the English curriculum. A curriculum coverage chart is available to download from the Schofield & Sims website. An extended glossary can also be found at the back of this teacher's guide [pages 91–92], with a full list of all the terminology relevant to the Year 1 curriculum, along with clear explanations, examples and lesson references.

IMPLEMENTING THE TEACHING MODEL

The **Grammar 1 Teacher's Guide** supports explicit teaching of grammar and punctuation within the wider teaching of reading, writing and speaking. It is based on focused teaching sessions, using the following pedagogical model:

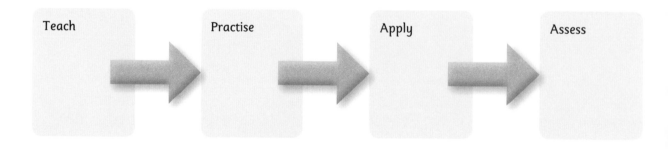

| Teach | Practise | Apply | Assess |

This teacher's guide supports an approach to teaching grammar and punctuation that is systematic, thorough and direct. It provides you with detailed **Teaching notes** for each lesson. A sample page is included below to show the structure of a typical lesson.

Teaching notes   Schofield & Sims **Grammar and Punctuation** | Grammar 1 Teacher's Guide

Lesson 1   Words and sentences

Focus   combining words to make sentences; separating words with spaces

Key terms   **word, sentence**

Focus text   Jack went to the party.
I went for a run.

TEACH

Show the first sentence of the focus text. Read it together, pointing to the words; say each word clearly. Discuss what the sentence tells us [e.g. Who is it about? What did he do?]. Repeat with the second sentence.

Cut the sentences from the first part of the photocopy master on the opposite page into separate words and mix them up. Ask: Can you remember the sentence about Jack? Say it together, pronouncing each word clearly. Count the words on your fingers. Involve the children in building the sentence, finding each word in turn and putting it in place. As you do this, draw attention to the spaces you leave between the words. Keep saying the sentence as you build it. When the sentence is complete, read it together to check it is complete.

Repeat the activity with the second sentence or make up a new sentence [e.g. Jack went for a run.].

Explain that you have been making sentences. Sentences are made up of words, which we put in order, to say something. When we write, we put words into sentences. When we write a sentence, we leave spaces between the words so it is easy to read.

Point out that the sentences you have made start with a capital letter and end with a full stop. [Note: This is the focus of the next lesson, Lesson 2.]

Sentences make sense and tell us something. Use the focus text words to make a sentence with a missing word or with words in the wrong order [e.g. I went run.]. Show that it does not make sense.

ACTIVITY   Provide the children with a sentence and a set of words from the second part of the photocopy master on the opposite page. Help them read and then rebuild the complete sentence using the cut-out words. Then ask them to make more sentences by changing one word from the set.

EXTEND   Discuss adding an extra word into a sentence to give more detail [e.g. I went for a long run.].

PRACTISE

Pupil book pages 4–5

APPLY

- Always ask the children to compose sentences orally before writing them.
- Compose sentences in a circle with each child adding one word to the sentence.
- The children use word banks or word cards to build sentences before writing them down.
- The children make simple books using repeated sentence stems [e.g. I like ...; I can ...].
- Write a short sentence from a familiar story on to a strip of card. Cut it up into words for the children to rebuild. Do the same with the children's own sentences.

ASSESS

Dictation: I get in the car.
Say: Put a full stop at the end of your sentence.
Check: The sentence is complete [no missing words] and spaces have been left between the words.

10

Annotation labels:

- The learning objective of the lesson.
- Terminology that the children will encounter in the lesson.
- A short focus text for use at the start of the lesson.
- Detailed lesson notes offering guidance on how to teach a specific grammatical feature or concept.
- Instructions for a fun activity based around the lesson.
- Extension of the lesson focus for children who want to explore further.
- Reference to the relevant pupil book pages, which contain practice activities to develop understanding.
- A dictation activity to assess learning.
- Ideas and activities for applying the concept in speech and independent writing.

TEACH

Each lesson begins with an introductory panel featuring the following information:

- **Focus** – The focus of the lesson is clearly stated.
- **Key terms** – The key terminology to be used in the teaching session is listed. Any new terminology that the children will come across for the first time in that lesson is highlighted in bold.
- **Focus text** – A short focus text is provided that has been designed for use at the start of the lesson. It is intended that the focus text is written or projected on to a whiteboard to be shared with the children. The focus texts cover a range of genres of writing and help to provide a context for the learning that allows the children to appreciate the purpose or effect of the target grammar or punctuation feature. All the focus texts are available to download from the Schofield & Sims website.

Clear guidance is given on how to use the **Focus text** at the start of the lesson to 'focus in' on the particular grammar or punctuation feature that you are teaching. The **Teaching notes** suggest possible ways that you can explain, demonstrate and discuss the feature to develop understanding. Sessions often involve some oral composition or shared writing, with the children involved in suggesting ideas and correcting mistakes.

In the **Grammar 1 Teacher's Guide** there is also an **Activity** for each lesson, based around a photocopy master. These activities are designed to be delivered orally and made into a fun game. The activity is a good way to check the children's understanding before they begin work in the pupil book or to refresh their memory before completing the second page of practice in the pupil book on another occasion.

The main teaching session covers the objectives that are required for the children to work at the expected standard, but there is also a suggestion for how you can **Extend** the focus for children who have grasped the main concept and are ready to delve deeper. These suggestions often provide a bridge to later lessons in the programme.

PRACTISE

Following the teaching session, the children are ready to practise the grammar or punctuation feature that has been introduced and clear page references are provided for the corresponding lesson in the pupil book. This provides the children with rich practice activities to consolidate their learning. The children can work individually or in pairs. In paired work, discussion between partners can help to develop understanding, encourage thoughtful answers and promote oral rehearsal.

At the top of each pupil book page, a **Remember** panel provides a child-friendly summary of a key learning point from the lesson, with examples that refer back to the **Focus text**. This acts as a reminder for the child and is also a useful reference for parents if sections of the pupil book are set as homework.

In **Grammar 1**, there are five pupil book activities for each lesson. As there are fewer statutory requirements in Year 1, additional practice is provided to give children a solid foundation in the building blocks of grammar: word and sentence formation. The activities are spread over two pages and do not need to be attempted all at the same time. They could be split out over a number of days, or sections could be set as homework. The **Try it** activities on the first page are simple activities designed to check understanding of the key learning point. The **More practice** activities on the second page develop this understanding further. You could do some of the activities orally, with the class or in groups, before the children write their answers. Each lesson then ends with a **Sentence practice** activity where the children compose their own sentence or sentences using the concept that has been taught in the lesson. A sample page spread from the pupil book is provided on page 7. It shows the structure of a typical page and some of the main features.

As the pupil book is completed, it will form an ongoing record of the child's progress. It will also be a useful reminder for the child when writing independently.

Answers to all the pupil book activities are provided in the teacher's guide. Alongside the answers you will also find detailed annotations offering guidance on what to look out for and how to tackle potential problems, as well as suggestions for discussing or comparing the children's answers.

There are **Revision** pages at the end of each section of the pupil book. In **Grammar 1**, these pages revise concepts introduced in earlier sections of the book, making sure that learning is not forgotten. In later books in the series the revision pages will also include revision of concepts from previous years. The focus of each revision activity is given on the **Answers** pages in the teacher's guide to help you identify areas where the children might need further revision.

Try it activities check for basic understanding of the key learning point.

The **Remember** panels provide a child-friendly summary of the key learning point.

Examples are given that refer back to the **Focus text**.

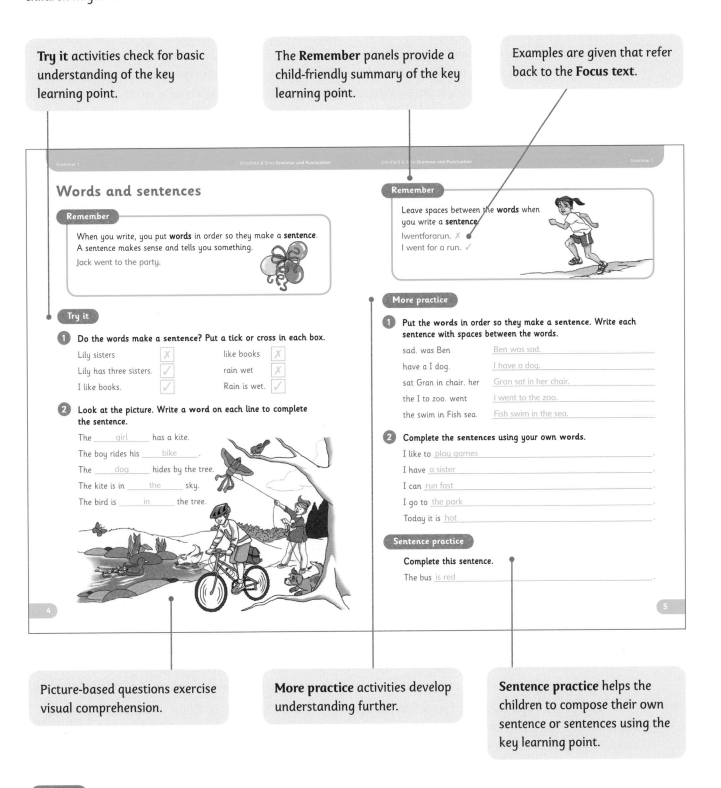

Picture-based questions exercise visual comprehension.

More practice activities develop understanding further.

Sentence practice helps the children to compose their own sentence or sentences using the key learning point.

APPLY

A challenge when teaching grammar and punctuation is ensuring that children transfer learning from grammar lessons into their own writing. This is why the **Teaching notes** always provide a list of suggestions for activities where the children might apply their new learning in written, or sometimes oral, composition. These opportunities may be in English lessons or across the curriculum. You can use these suggestions as and when appropriate and you should also look for opportunities to embed learning in the writing activities you already have planned.

It is important to establish the expectation that what has been taught and practised in a grammar and punctuation lesson is applied when writing. This can be helped by setting targets for writing that relate to a specific grammar and punctuation concept that has been taught, and referring to these before, during and after writing, especially in marking and feedback. You will find further support for target-setting on page 9.

At the end of each section of the pupil book there is a short **Writing task.** This again helps to make explicit the link between the grammar and punctuation lessons and the children's own writing. The task provides an opportunity for the children to apply, or 'show off', what they have learnt about grammar and punctuation by using it in written composition. It can be used as a starting point for further creative writing or topic-based activities. There is more information below about how to use and assess the **Writing task**.

ASSESS

Regular assessment is crucial to check understanding, reflect on learning and monitor progress. It is important that teachers know what the children have learnt, what they are finding difficult and what they need to know next. This helps inform teaching, planning and target-setting. **Grammar 1** and its related **Teacher's Guide** offer frequent opportunities and a range of resources for in-school assessment, which can be used flexibly in line with your own school's assessment policy.

Ongoing assessment

At the end of each page of the **Teaching notes** you will find a short assessment task based around a dictation exercise. This is designed to be used once the children have completed the relevant lesson in the pupil book and begun to apply the new learning in their writing. The children are required to write and punctuate a dictated sentence or sentences. They are often then asked to change or annotate the sentence in some way, following verbal prompts. This dictation task is designed to show whether the children have understood the terminology and the key learning objective of the lesson. Sometimes previous learning is also checked. A **Dictation assessment sheet** is available to download from the Schofield & Sims website.

Periodic assessment

The **Writing task** at the end of each section in the pupil book allows for a more formal assessment of how the children are applying their cumulative knowledge of sentence structure, grammar and punctuation in their own writing.

At Key Stage 1, you should introduce and discuss the task with the children before they begin writing. You may feel that some tasks need more of an introduction than others [e.g. discussing ideas if the children are asked to write an imaginary sequence of events]. You should not, however, orally rehearse sentences that the children might write, as putting ideas into complete sentences is part of the assessment.

Included in the teacher's guide is an **Analysis sheet** for each **Writing task** [pages 32, 56 and 80]. This lists relevant criteria relating to punctuation, and to grammar and sentence structure based on what has been taught to date. Look for each criterion in the child's completed **Writing task** and record whether there is no evidence, some evidence or clear evidence of the use of that feature in the piece of writing. Photocopies of these sheets can also be used to analyse other samples of writing to give a better picture of a child's abilities.

Also included is a **Pupil checklist** for each **Writing task** [pages 33, 57 and 81]. This is designed to encourage the children's self-assessment and also allows you to give targeted feedback. As the children complete the checklist you could ask them to annotate their writing to show where they have successfully used a particular grammar or punctuation feature [e.g. circling the capital letters they have used].

Whether you choose to use the **Analysis sheet** or the **Pupil checklist**, both include a space for you to record a future target for the child. This is an important part of the writing assessments: identifying strengths and weaknesses and informing future teaching. Any problems or misunderstandings that are noted should be addressed and targets updated based on the evidence.

Summative assessment

There is a **Final test** provided as a photocopiable resource on pages 82–85 of this teacher's guide. This is designed to be used as an end-of-year assessment when all or most of the sections of the pupil book are complete. It is similar in style to the short answer test in the end of Key Stage 1 National Tests and it covers all the content introduced in the programme so far. You can use it to help check the children's learning and whether their progress is in line with expectations.

A **Mark scheme** for the **Final test** is provided on pages 86–87 and gives the answers and assessment focus of each question. The **Analysis sheet** for the **Final test** allows you to record the pupils' marks and will be helpful in identifying individual or class strengths and areas that might need to be revisited. This can be found on page 88 and a whole-class version is available to download from the Schofield & Sims website.

Tracking progress

A number of resources are provided at the back of the teacher's guide and as downloadable resources to further support assessment of learning, tracking progress and record-keeping.

Following a **Writing task**, if a group of children require further focused support on a particular writing target, the **Target tracking sheet** on page 89 can be used to note evidence of progress towards that target. You should look for evidence of progress in independent writing in English and in other subjects. Judgements should not be made solely on one piece of writing.

Pupil name	Evidence from independent writing	Progress in independent writing
Sarah Jacobs	Paragraph on 'My family'. Book review of 'The Nightingale'. Science report on 'Habitats'.	① ② ③

The target should be reviewed after a set period of time to see if it has been achieved. A new target might then be set, or further teaching and reinforcement opportunities planned as necessary. A **Pupil target reminder** is available to download from the Schofield & Sims website. This can be placed on a child's desk as a prompt to remind them of their current writing target.

The **Learning pathways sheet** on page 90 acts as an at-a-glance overview of where a child is in their learning. If completed at regular intervals [e.g. at the end of every term] it allows you to track the progress that has been made and to identify areas where further support might be needed. Alternatively it can be completed just once at the end of the year to act as a useful summative record for the child's subsequent teacher. The chart shows criteria in line with the expected standards for Year 1. Circles are ticked to show the depth of the child's understanding. These judgements should be made using a variety of evidence, including a number of examples of independent writing. Learning is only definitely embedded when the concept is always or nearly always present based on evidence from a range of writing tasks. A **Learning pathways class chart**, available to download from the Schofield & Sims website, allows you to keep a record of progress for the whole class in one spreadsheet.

The children should also be encouraged to reflect on their own learning at regular intervals, saying what they have learnt and how they have used it in their writing. There is a **Progress chart** at the back of the pupil book where the children can record their progress through the programme by ticking the circle when they feel they have achieved the content of the statement.

Lesson 1 Words and sentences

Focus combining words to make sentences; separating words with spaces

Key terms **word, sentence**

Focus text Jack went to the party.
I went for a run.

TEACH

Show the first sentence of the focus text. Read it together, pointing to the words; say each word clearly. Discuss what the sentence tells us [e.g. Who is it about? What did he do?]. Repeat with the second sentence.

Cut the sentences from the first part of the photocopy master on the opposite page into separate words and mix them up. Ask: Can you remember the sentence about Jack? Say it together, pronouncing each word clearly. Count the words on your fingers. Involve the children in building the sentence, finding each word in turn and putting it in place. As you do this, draw attention to the spaces you leave between the words. Keep saying the sentence as you build it. When the sentence is complete, read it together to check it is complete.

Repeat the activity with the second sentence or make up a new sentence [e.g. Jack went for a run.].

Explain that you have been making sentences. Sentences are made up of words, which we put in order, to say something. When we write, we put words into sentences. When we write a sentence, we leave spaces between the words so it is easy to read.

Point out that the sentences you have made start with a capital letter and end with a full stop. [Note: This is the focus of the next lesson, Lesson 2.]

Sentences make sense and tell us something. Use the focus text words to make a sentence with a missing word or with words in the wrong order [e.g. I went run.]. Show that it does not make sense.

ACTIVITY Provide the children with a sentence and a set of words from the second part of the photocopy master on the opposite page. Help them read and then rebuild the complete sentence using the cut-out words. Then ask them to make more sentences by changing one word from the set.

EXTEND Discuss adding an extra word into a sentence to give more detail [e.g. I went for a long run.].

PRACTISE

Pupil book pages 4–5

APPLY

- Always ask the children to compose sentences orally before writing them.
- Compose sentences in a circle with each child adding one word to the sentence.
- The children use word banks or word cards to build sentences before writing them down.
- The children make simple books using repeated sentence stems [e.g. I like ...; I can ...].
- Write a short sentence from a familiar story on to a strip of card. Cut it up into words for the children to rebuild. Do the same with the children's own sentences.

ASSESS

Dictation: I get in the car.
Say: Put a full stop at the end of your sentence.
Check: The sentence is complete [no missing words] and spaces have been left between the words.

Cut the sentence into words. Then rebuild it.

Jack	went	to	the	party.
I	went	for	a	run.

Cut the sentence into words. Then rebuild it. Change one word to make a new sentence.

I	like	to	run.
swim.	skip.	sing.	jump.

Ben	went	to	bed.
sleep.	play.	town.	help.

Ellie	lost	her	glove.
book.	coat.	way.	hat.

I	saw	a	car.
snail.	film.	crab.	robin.

Grace	went	to	the	shop.
seaside.	zoo.	park.	bank.	

From: **Grammar 1 Teacher's Guide** © *Schofield & Sims Ltd, 2017. This page may be photocopied after purchase.*

Pupil book answers

Words and sentences

Remember

When you write, you put **words** in order so they make a **sentence**.
A sentence makes sense and tells you something.

Jack went to the party.

Try it

The children should choose words to create sentences to describe what is happening in the picture. The sentences should make sense. [The bird could be 'in' or 'on' the tree.]

With questions based around a picture, you could talk about the events in the picture beforehand. For example, here you could talk about what is happening in the picture and use language such as 'by the tree', 'in the sky'.

1 Do the words make a **sentence**? Put a tick or cross in each box.

Lily sisters   X   like books   X

Lily has three sisters. ✓   rain wet   X

I like books. ✓   Rain is wet. ✓

2 Look at the picture. Write a **word** on each line to complete the sentence.

The _____girl_____ has a kite.

The boy rides his _____bike_____ .

The _____dog_____ hides by the tree.

The kite is in _____the_____ sky.

The bird is _____in_____ the tree.

4

Schofield & Sims **Grammar and Punctuation**   Grammar 1

Remember

Leave spaces between the **words** when you write a **sentence**.

Iwentforarun. ✗
I went for a run. ✓

Check that the spaces between words are a reasonable size.

Although the focus is on ordering words to form a sentence, the sentences should have capital letters and full stops if the children have copied the words correctly from the question.

More practice

1. Put the **words** in order so they make a **sentence**. Write each sentence with spaces between the words.

sad. was Ben	Ben was sad.
have a I dog.	I have a dog.
sat Gran in chair. her	Gran sat in her chair.
the I to zoo. went	I went to the zoo.
the swim in Fish sea.	Fish swim in the sea.

These are just examples of how the sentences might be completed. Any sentence that makes sense is acceptable. Ask the children to read their sentences aloud so they can compare them.

Where more than one word is added there should be a reasonable space between the words.

2. Complete the **sentences** using your own **words**.

I like to play games .

I have a sister .

I can run fast .

I go to the park .

Today it is hot .

Sentence practice

Complete this sentence.

The bus is red .

5

This is just an example of how the sentence might be completed. Any sentence that makes sense is acceptable.

There should be reasonable spaces between the words.

A full stop is given at the end of the line but the children may add their own full stop at the end of the sentence. [Note: Full stops and capital letters are the focus of the next lesson, Lesson 2.]

Lesson 2 Capital letters and full stops

Focus using capital letters and full stops to demarcate sentences

Key terms word, sentence, **capital letter**, **full stop**

Focus text **the little man ran away**

TEACH

Show the focus text and read it aloud. Discuss what it tells us. Ask: Is this a sentence? Are the words in the right order? Does it make sense and tell us something? Is it complete or is there something missing? Some of the children might notice there is no capital letter or full stop.

Explain that all sentences must start with a capital letter and end with a full stop. These are important signals to the reader: the capital letter tells the reader 'this is the start of the sentence'; the full stop tells the reader 'this is the end of the sentence'.

Point to the first letter of the sentence in the focus text. Ask the children to show you a capital 'T' by making it with their fingers or writing it in the air. In colour, change the first letter to a capital 'T'. Read the sentence and ask what needs to go after the last word. Add the full stop in colour.

Young children will often use capital letters *within* words. Explain that capital letters are 'special letters' only used at the *start* of special words, such as the first word of a sentence.

Say another sentence to follow the focus sentence [e.g. He ran down the road.]. Say the sentence a few times together. Ask the children to raise their hands to signal the start of the sentence and to make a fist to signal the end of the sentence. Now write the sentence with the capital letter and full stop shown in colour. As you do so, ask the children to show what a capital 'H' looks like and to make a fist to remind you to put the full stop at the end.

ACTIVITY Give the children some parts of a sentence from the photocopy master on the opposite page. Ask them to make a sentence and to then say it, raising their hands to signal the capital letter and making a fist to signal the full stop.

EXTEND Extend the sentences you write, discussing where the full stop goes now [e.g. The little man ran away from the big dog.].

PRACTISE

Pupil book pages 6–7

APPLY

- When orally rehearsing sentences, the children continue to use the signals of raising a hand to represent a capital letter and clenching a fist for the full stop.
- Use different colours to show capital letters and full stops in sentences displayed around the classroom. Ask the children to highlight the capital letters and full stops in sentences they write.
- Provide lots of opportunities for the children to write one sentence [e.g. to go with a picture or about an activity or event]. Remind them to use a capital letter and a full stop.

ASSESS

Dictation: The boy went to town.
Check: The sentence starts with a capital letter and ends with a full stop. The sentence is written correctly with clear spaces and no words are missing.

Make a sentence. Then write your sentence. Begin it with a capital letter and end it with a full stop.

the girl	sat	in the tree
a boy	ran	away
my friend	made	a cake
my dad	hid	outside
this man	ate	our dinner
your cat	was	by the shed
the big dog	saw	the bin
a bird	sang	to me

Pupil book answers

Capital letters and full stops

Remember

A **sentence** must start with a **capital letter** and end with a **full stop**.

The little man ran away.

The capital letters at the start of the sentences should be the correct shape and be the same height as the ascenders [i.e. clearly taller than the letters without ascenders, as in the word 'We' in the second sentence].

Check that there are no capital letters used *within* the sentence. However, some of the children may have used a capital letter for 'Mum', as they are more used to writing the word like this. There is no need to mark this as incorrect.

Check also that there are clear spaces between words.

Try it

1　Does the sentence have a **capital letter** at the start and a **full stop** at the end? Put a tick or cross in each box.

it is hot today.　　　　　　　X
The ducks began to quack　　X
A van went up the hill.　　　　✓
My coat is blue.　　　　　　　✓
there are seven days in a week　X
We like to paint.　　　　　　　✓

2　Write each **sentence** so it starts with a **capital letter** and ends with a **full stop**.

a dog can bark　　　　　A dog can bark.
we need food to eat　　　We need food to eat.
you can play here　　　　You can play here.
the man was rich　　　　The man was rich.
it is cold today　　　　　It is cold today.
my mum made a cake　　My mum made a cake.

6

Remember

When you write a **sentence**, put a **capital letter** at the start and a **full stop** at the end.

More practice

1 Look at the picture and write the start of each **sentence**. Remember to start with a **capital letter**.

A hen is pecking corn.   _Cows_ are eating grass.

The dog is by the gate.   _The farmer_ has a bucket.

2 Write the end of each **sentence**. Remember to end with a **full stop**.

Starfish live in _the sea._

A bird is singing in _the tree._

The sun is _up in the sky._

You can go sailing in _a boat._

Sentence practice

Write a sentence about a bike. Remember the **capital letter** and **full stop**.

My bike is red.

7

The sentences do not have to start exactly as shown here, as long as they make sense and correspond to the picture [e.g. it could be 'The hen' rather than 'A hen', or 'A man' rather than 'The farmer']. The children need to add in the subject of the sentence – who it is about.

Again, check that capital letters are the correct shape, the same height as ascenders and taller than letters without ascenders. Work on this in handwriting.

The sentences do not have to end as shown here but they must make sense and have no missing words, as well as having full stops [e.g. 'A bird is singing in tree.' does not make sense]. Ask the children to read their sentences aloud to check that they make sense. Compare their different endings.

Again, check the spacing between the added words.

This is an example of a possible sentence. It must make sense, have clear spaces between words, start with a capital letter and end with a full stop.

Check that there are no capital letters used _within_ the sentence.

Lesson 3 Capital letters: names and 'I'

Focus using capital letters for people's names and the word 'I'

Key terms capital letter, word, sentence

Focus text Beth played football with Joe and Evie.
Alex and I played football with Vikram and Jodie.

TEACH

Show the first sentence of the focus text and read it aloud. Discuss who played football. Underline the three names [Beth, Joe, Evie]. Ask: What do you notice about the first letter of all these words? [they are capital letters]

Show the second sentence and read it aloud. Discuss who played football this time. Underline the three names and the word 'I'. Ask: What do you notice about these words? [e.g. the names begin with capital letters; the word 'I' is also a capital letter]

Remind the children that capital letters are only used at the start of special words such as the first word in a sentence. Explain that people's names are also special words so they always start with a capital letter, even if they are not at the start of a sentence.

Explain that the word 'I' is another special word because it is how we talk about ourselves. The word 'I' is always a capital letter even if it is not at the start of the sentence.

Together, compose some more sentences using names and 'I' [e.g. Ali and I worked with Kate and Emma.].

ACTIVITY Play a game with the word cards from the photocopy master on the opposite page. Hold each word up in turn and ask the children to shout 'capital letter' when they see a name. Add the capital letters and stick the names on a special 'names' board. Let the children write their own names on stickers and add them to the display.

EXTEND Introduce capital letters for titles [Mr, Mrs, Miss, Ms], place names and days of the week. [Note: This is the focus of Lesson 7.]

PRACTISE

Pupil book pages 8–9

APPLY

- The children write about characters in stories. Remind them to use capital letters for the names.
- The children write about events or personal experiences, using capital letters for 'I' as well as names [e.g. I lost my ...; I felt ...].
- Help the children to write name labels for trays, coat pegs and folders, with the capital letters in bright colours.
- Write captions for photos of the children [e.g. doing different activities] using their names, and display them around the classroom.
- Together, count how many capital letters the children use when writing about themselves, their friends or family.

ASSESS

Dictation: Mum said I can help Ted.
Say: You should have three words starting with a capital letter. Underline them.
Check: The capital letters are the correct shape and size. The sentence is written correctly, with clear spaces and a full stop at the end.

Cut out the name cards. Add a capital letter to the start of the names.

boy	ali	harry
girl	oscar	charlie
dog	emma	yasmin
cat	josh	wayne
rabbit	kate	amy
sister	louis	rosa
brother	sita	bella
friend	daniel	grace

Pupil book answers

Capital letters: names and 'I'

Remember

Always put a **capital letter** at the start of someone's name.

Beth played football with Joe and Evie.

Try it

1 Circle the **capital letter** at the start of every name you can see.

Sam has a dog called Benny.

Tanya plays ball with Ella.

Harry and Chris go to Adam's party.

Marlon likes to read with his friend James.

One day Poppy went to visit Nisha.

> The capital letter at the start of 'One' should *not* be circled as it is not at the start of a name.

2 Look at the pictures. Add a name to complete each caption. Remember the **capital letter**.

> The children can choose any names for this activity but they must begin with a capital letter.
>
> Capital letters should be the correct shape and height.

my dog ___Benny___   my cat ___Jess___

This is ___Madel___ .   my friend ___Sam___

8

Remember

You use the word 'I' to write about yourself. The word 'I' is always a **capital letter**.

Alex and I played football with Vikram and Jodie.

More practice

1 Underline the words that need a **capital letter**. Then write each sentence correctly.

i think i can do it.   I think I can do it.

dad said i can help.   Dad said I can help.

i went to see emma.   I went to see Emma.

ellie and i saw jake.   Ellie and I saw Jake.

now i must find luke.   Now I must find Luke.

Check that the sentences also end with a full stop.

2 Complete each sentence. Use a name or the word 'I'. Remember the **capital letter**.

_____Nina_____ is my best friend.

_____I_____ can run fast.

Simon and _____I_____ like playing pirates.

I sit next to _____Oliver_____ .

This morning _____I_____ was late for school.

The children can use names or the word 'I' in these sentences as long as they make sense [e.g. 'I is my best friend.' is not acceptable as it does not make sense].

Encourage the children to read their sentences aloud to check that they make sense.

Sentence practice

Write a sentence that needs <u>two</u> **capital letters** in it.

I went to the beach with Rory.

9

This is an example of the sort of sentence the children might write. There must be a capital letter at the start of the sentence, whether it is part of a name or not. The other capital letter can be for a name or the word 'I'.

Check that the sentence makes sense and ends with a full stop.

Lesson 4 Making up sentences

Focus orally composing and writing complete sentences

Key terms sentence, word, capital letter, full stop

Focus text I go to the park with Mum.
Play swings.
An ice cream.

TEACH

Display the focus text. Read each line in turn and discuss whether it is a sentence. Ask: Why? Why not? Recap the children's understanding of the term 'sentence' [e.g. it must make sense; be complete; tell us something; and have a capital letter and full stop]. Although the second and third lines of the focus text include ideas, capital letters and full stops, they are not complete sentences.

Invite the children to suggest how the second line could be made into a complete sentence [e.g. I like to play on the swings.]. Say the sentence twice and count the words on your fingers. Ask the children to say the sentence as you write it. Pause after 'swings' to see if the children remind you to put a full stop. Read the complete sentence to check that it makes sense and nothing has been left out.

Do the same with the third line, making it into a complete sentence [e.g. We had an ice cream.]. You could miss out a word as you write it and see if the children notice. If not, draw attention to the missing word as you read the complete sentence.

Explain that when we write, we put our ideas into complete sentences. We do this by *thinking* of an idea, *saying* the complete sentence aloud, *writing* it word by word and then *reading* it to check that it makes sense and nothing has been missed out.

ACTIVITY Give each pair of children a picture from the photocopy master on the opposite page. Ask them to *think* of a sentence and to *say* it a few times. Listen to the sentences with everyone raising their hands to show the capital letter and making a fist to show the full stop. Ask the children to then *write* their sentence, *read* it and *check* it.

EXTEND Look at how you could extend the sentences [e.g. We had a strawberry ice cream. We had an ice cream cone.].

PRACTISE

Pupil book pages 10–11

APPLY

- Use 'writing partners' to encourage the children to orally compose sentences before writing them.
- The children orally compose and write one or two complete sentences to accompany pictures or photos.
- Use sequences of pictures to prompt a series of sentences to recount an event or a story.
- Across the curriculum, provide opportunities for the children to orally compose and write sentences [e.g. in science, write sentences to say what things are made from].
- Together, orally compose and write some sentences for a display [e.g. about an object – 'This is a …'].
- Use sentences from stories or other texts as models for the children to write their own sentences.

ASSESS

Dictation: We went to the pond.
Say: Write another sentence to follow this one. Say it, write it, check it.
Check: Both sentences are complete and have capital letters and full stops.
Answer: e.g. I fed the ducks.

Choose a picture. Make up a sentence about the picture. Say the
sentence. Write it. Check it.

Pupil book answers

Making up sentences

Remember

When you write, you put your ideas into **sentences**. It helps to say the sentence aloud before you write it.

I like to play on the swings.

> These are just examples of how the words might be used in a complete sentence.
>
> The sentences must make sense, have clear spaces between words and start with a capital letter and end with a full stop.

Try it

1 Add some **words** to make these words into a **sentence**. Say each sentence, then write it.

mum shopping   Mum went shopping.

we play garden   We like to play in the garden.

boy sand   A boy digs in the sand.

house green door   My house has a green door.

fox den   The fox was in his den.

2 Look at the picture. Write <u>three</u> **sentences** about it. Say each sentence before you write it.

Mum is in her chair.

The girl has a rocket.

The dog is barking at the rocket.

These are just examples of sentences the children might write. The sentences should describe events that are happening in the picture. Encourage the children to say and improve their sentences before writing them. Compare the children's sentences. Some of them may write longer sentences with more detail [e.g. The lady is sitting in her armchair].

The sentences should make sense, have clear spaces between words and start with a capital letter and end with a full stop.

Remember

When you finish writing a **sentence**, read it. Check it makes sense and is complete.

> Discuss with the children why they put a cross by some sentences [Was it a missing word or a missing full stop?].
>
> Let the children be 'the teacher' and use a red/green colouring pencil to correct the sentences they marked as incorrect.

More practice

1 Read each **sentence**. Put a tick in the box if the sentence makes sense and is complete. Put a cross if there is something missing.

Mum broke a cup. ✓

Jenny gave me a present ✗

The boys play with car. ✗

I saw a bee a flower. ✗

Molly came to play. ✓

The girl put her red shoes. ✗

2 Complete each **sentence**.

I like to _play with my friends._

I want to _go swimming._

Today I saw _a fire engine._

My house _has a green door._

Some dogs _are big._

> The children can choose how to end these sentences. These are just examples. The sentences must make sense and end with a full stop.
>
> If they do not, remind the children to read the sentence aloud to check that it makes sense, or to check whether they have forgotten anything.

Sentence practice

Write a sentence with these <u>two</u> **words** in it.

truck   road

There is a big truck in the road.

> This is just an example. The sentence must make sense, start with a capital letter, end with a full stop and have clear spaces between the words.
>
> Remind the children to follow the process: *think* of a sentence, *say* it, *write* it and then *read* it to check that it makes sense and is complete.

Lesson 5 Using 'and' to join words

> **Focus** using 'and' to join words
>
> **Key terms** word, **joining word**
>
> **Focus text** Mr Bradshaw painted all the shops and houses. He painted them yellow and green and pink and blue. All the people stopped and stared.

TEACH

Show the focus text and read it aloud. Ask: What did Mr Bradshaw paint? [shops and houses] What colours did he use? [yellow and green and pink and blue] What did the people do? [stopped and stared] Underline these words, pointing out that they are joined by 'and'.

Explain that the word 'and' is a joining word. We can use it to join two or more words. Look at the examples in the focus text. In the first sentence, 'and' is used to join two things [shops and houses]. In the second sentence, 'and' joins together a list of colour words [yellow, green, pink and blue]. In the third sentence, 'and' joins two actions [stopped and stared].

With the children, compose more sentences for the focus text using 'and' to join other words, such as two more things that Mr Bradshaw might paint [e.g. He painted the walls and fences.]; other colours he might use [e.g. He painted them red and orange.]; or other actions or reactions [e.g. People came and watched.]. Say or write the sentences with the children making a fist to show the full stop at the end of the sentence.

ACTIVITY In small groups, the children play 'find a pair' using the words from the photocopy master on the opposite page. They then read out the pairs they have made using 'and' [e.g. Jack and Jill] or use the pairs in sentences.

EXTEND Show how 'and' can be used to join longer phrases [e.g. the little old man and the little old woman] or to join two short sentences [e.g. Mr Bradshaw painted and the people watched.]. [Note: Joining sentences is the focus of Lesson 6.]

PRACTISE

Pupil book pages 12–13

APPLY

- The children write captions for pictures or photos of two people [e.g. Archie and Sam fed the chickens.].
- Across the curriculum, use 'and' to join two words when working on topics such as properties of materials [e.g. The spoon is smooth and shiny.]; or the weather [e.g. Today it is wet and windy.].
- Together, look for 'and' in story titles [e.g. Goldilocks and the Three Bears; The Princess and the Pea; Jack and the Beanstalk]. Then invent some of your own [e.g. Goldilocks and the Three Elephants].
- In stories, look for examples of sentences using 'and' to join words [e.g. Elmer was yellow and orange and red and pink ...; It grew and grew and grew.]. Use these as models for the children to write their own sentences.
- Write captions for displays of items using 'and' [e.g. shells and pebbles; red and green leaves].

ASSESS

Dictation: We had chicken and chips.
Say: Use 'and' to add something else after 'chips'.
Check: The new sentence is correctly punctuated with one full stop and capital letter. The full stop must be moved to the end of the sentence [i.e. not '... chips. And peas.'].
Answer: e.g. We had chicken and chips and peas.

Cut up the word cards. Find a pair to join with 'and'.

Jack	Jill
Batman	Robin
brother	sister
king	queen
cats	dogs
Mum	Dad
boys	girls
snakes	ladders

Pupil book answers

Using 'and' to join words

Remember

The word '**and**' is a **joining word**. You can use 'and' to join **words** together.

shops and houses   yellow and green

Try it

1 Use the word '**and**' to join these words together.

jelly ___and___ ice cream

Mum ___and___ Dad

bread ___and___ butter

arms ___and___ legs

girl ___and___ boy

hot ___and___ cold

hide ___and___ seek

you ___and___ me

2 Look at the picture. Complete the sentence, using '**and**' to join on another **word**.

It is hot _and sunny._

Dad eats fish _and chips._

The girls play bat _and ball._

Owen has a bucket _and spade._

Dad took off his shoes _and socks._

The children should choose words suggested by the picture.

Check that 'and' is written with a lower-case 'a', not a capital 'A'.

Check that a full stop has been added to the end of each sentence.

12

Remember

You can use '**and**' to join words in a **sentence**.

He painted the shops and houses yellow and green.
People stopped and stared.

Check that the word 'and' has been added in the correct position.

Check also that the sentences begin with a capital letter, end with a full stop and have clear spacing between words.

More practice

1 The word '**and**' is missing from these sentences. Write each sentence correctly.

Let us wait see.   Let us wait and see.

He began to huff puff.   He began to huff and puff.

They ran ran.   They ran and ran.

Rabbits can hop jump.   Rabbits can hop and jump.

He sat down cried.   He sat down and cried.

These are just examples. Other answers are acceptable as long as they make sense and use 'and' to join another word or words [e.g. He jumped up and ran away. The woman put on her hat and scarf. Josie has a brother and two sisters.]. Discuss the different endings the children have written.

Check that a full stop has been added at the end of each sentence.

2 Complete the sentence using '**and**' and another **word** or words.

Josie has a brother and sister.

He jumped up and down.

Today it is cold and wet.

The woman put on her hat and coat.

The farmer fed the sheep and the cows.

The flowers are red and yellow.

Sentence practice

Write a sentence about <u>two</u> things you can see right now. Use the word '**and**' in your sentence.

I can see lots of boys and girls.

13

This is an example of a possible sentence. The sentence must make sense and use 'and' to join two words.

Check that the sentence has a capital letter and a full stop in the correct position.

Revision 1 answers

Focus: combining words to make sentences; separating words with spaces

Check that the spaces between words are a reasonable size.

The sentences should begin with a capital letter and end with a full stop, as these are given in the question.

These pages revise concepts introduced in Section 1. The focus of each activity is given to help identify areas where the children might need further revision.

Grammar 1   Schofield & Sims **Grammar and Punctuation**

Revision 1

1 Put the **words** in order so they make a **sentence**.

is kitchen. in Dad the   Dad is in the kitchen.

rocks. hit the ship The   The ship hit the rocks.

car I outside. saw a   I saw a car outside.

Focus: using capital letters and full stops to demarcate sentences

Use this activity to remind the children to reread sentences to check for capital letters and full stops. Discuss why the other two sentences are not correct. Let the children 'be teacher' and put in the full stop or capital letter to correct them.

2 Check these **sentences**. Put a tick in the box if the sentence makes sense and is complete. Put a cross if there is something missing.

We slept in a tent. ✓

I need a pen ✗

I like to read a good book. ✓

the stars shine at night. ✗

3 Write these **sentences** correctly.

a scarf is made from wool   A scarf is made from wool.

the Man was in a rush   The man was in a rush.

Focus: using capital letters and full stops to demarcate sentences

In the second question, check that the capital 'M' at the start of 'Man' has been replaced with a lower-case 'm'.

4 There is a **word** missing from each **sentence**. Write the sentence correctly.

Dan has pet rabbit.   Dan has a pet rabbit.

In winter it cold.   In winter it is cold.

I see my brother sister.   I see my brother and sister.

14

Focus: checking sentences are complete

Use this activity to remind the children to reread their sentences to check that they make sense [e.g. no missing words].

Check also the sentence punctuation and the spacing between words.

5 Underline <u>three</u> **words** that need a **capital letter**. Write the words correctly.

Today <u>i</u> played with <u>lily</u> and <u>brett</u>.

    I   Lily   Brett

Focus: using capital letters for people's names and the word 'I'

The word 'Today' at the start of the sentence should not be underlined as it already has a capital letter.

6 Complete each **sentence** using <u>two</u> food ideas from the picture. Join your two words with '**and**'.

We grew <u>carrots and peas.</u>

I like <u>bread and jam.</u>

The shop sells <u>eggs and cheese.</u>

Dad needs <u>flour and milk.</u>

Focus: using 'and' to join words

The children can use different words to those shown here. It does not matter if the children use a word more than once or if they use their own ideas based loosely on the picture.

Check that capital letters are not used for 'and' or the added words.

15

Writing task 1: Analysis sheet

Tick the circles to show amount of evidence found in writing:
1 No evidence
2 Some evidence
3 Clear evidence

Pupil name: _____

Date: _____

Assessing punctuation

The writing sample demonstrates:	Evidence		
capital letters used at the beginning of sentences.	1	2	3
sentence boundaries recognised and demarcated with full stops.	1	2	3
capital letters used for 'I' and people's names [e.g. the friend's name].	1	2	3
capital letters used only where needed – no incorrect use [e.g. in the middle of words; for words other than names].	1	2	3

Assessing grammar and sentence structure

The writing sample demonstrates:	Evidence		
words formed into complete sentences.	1	2	3
grammatically correct sentences [e.g. no missing words].	1	2	3
appropriate spacing between words.	1	2	3
the word 'and' used to join two words or ideas [e.g. We like to sit and read.].	1	2	3

Key target: _____

Writing task 1: Pupil checklist

Name: _____   Date: _____

Reread what you have written to check that it makes sense. Tick the circle if you have correctly used the punctuation or grammar feature in your writing.

Punctuation

◯ I have used capital letters at the beginning of sentences.

◯ I have used full stops at the end of sentences.

◯ I have used capital letters for 'I' and for names.

Grammar and sentences

◯ I have said my ideas aloud before writing them.

◯ I have checked that my sentences make sense and are complete.

◯ I have left spaces between my words.

◯ I have used the word 'and' to join words or ideas in a sentence.

Teacher feedback

My key target: _____

_____

_____

Lesson 6 Using 'and' to join sentences

Focus joining sentences using 'and'

Key terms sentence, joining word, capital letter, full stop

Focus text **Leah had a kite. She flew it in the park. The kite flew away. It landed in the tree.**

TEACH

Display the focus text and read it aloud. Discuss what it tells us about Leah and what happened to her kite. Read it again. Ask: How many sentences are there? [four] Identify the capital letter and the full stop demarcating each sentence.

Explain that you will join two sentences together to make one longer sentence. Read the first two sentences and then say the new sentence: Leah had a kite *and* she flew it in the park. Insert the word 'and' into the focus text. Read the new sentence and make the necessary changes to the punctuation [crossing out the full stop after 'kite' and changing the capital letter 'S']. Point out that it is now one sentence so it needs only one capital letter and one full stop.

Explain that 'and' is a 'joining word'. It can be used to join two sentences together to make one longer sentence. [Note: The word 'and' is a conjunction but there is no need to introduce the term at this stage. Conjunctions are referred to as joining words in **Grammar 1** and 2.]

Ask the pupils to help you join the remaining two sentences in the focus text, using 'and'. Say the new sentence together, insert the word 'and' and change the punctuation. Since young writers will often put a full stop and start the next sentence 'And ...', make it clear that 'and' is a word we use to join ideas *within* a sentence.

ACTIVITY Give each child a sentence from the photocopy master on the opposite page. Ask them to find a partner with a sentence that could be joined to their sentence using 'and'. Listen to the new sentences. Ask the other children to raise a hand at the start of a sentence to represent the capital letter and to make a fist at the end to represent the full stop.

EXTEND Look at examples of the children's own writing and discuss when 'and' might be used to join two sentences, and when it is better to use separate sentences.

PRACTISE

Pupil book pages 18–19

APPLY

- When reading, collect examples of sentences using 'and'. Display these so the children can use them as models to write sentences of their own.
- The children draw pictures of events from stories and write a sentence using 'and' to describe two things that happened [e.g. The children curled up and they fell asleep.].
- When the children are orally composing sentences, prompt them by asking: And what happened next? [e.g. 'I went to the river ...' – And what did you do there?]. Then ask them to repeat the complete sentence with the two events joined by 'and'.

ASSESS

Dictation: Billy sits on the rocks and he looks for fish.

Check: The sentence is correctly punctuated with one capital letter and one full stop.

Cut out the sentences. Find two sentences to join together with the word 'and'. Say your new longer sentence and then write it.

The man falls over.	He lands in the mud.
The boy jumps in the pond.	He gets wet.
The dog runs away.	He hides in the woods.
The clown does a trick.	We all clap.
Dad sits down.	He falls asleep.
It starts to rain.	We all get wet.
James sings.	We all join in.
A snake escapes.	We all scream.

Pupil book answers

Using 'and' to join sentences

Remember

You can use the word '**and**' to join two **sentences** together.

Leah had a kite. She flew it in the park.   (2 sentences)

Leah had a kite and she flew it in the park.   (1 sentence)

Try it

1 Use the word '**and**' to join the two **sentences** together.
   Read each new sentence you make.

Amir fell over ____and____ he hurt his leg.

Tom ran away ____and____ he hid outside.

Molly went to bed ____and____ she fell asleep.

We went to the park ____and____ I played on the swings.

Max took his net ____and____ he went fishing.

I like cats ____and____ I like dogs.

These are just examples of how the sentences might be completed. The children can choose different ideas but the completed sentence must make sense and end with a full stop.

Ask the children to read aloud their sentences and discuss the different ways they have been completed.

2 Complete each **sentence** with your own **word** or words.

The man gets in the car and he goes _to work._

Mum has coffee and I have _milk._

I put on my coat and I go _out to play._

We went to the zoo and we saw _the tigers._

The sun is out and it _is hot._

18

36

Remember

When you use the word '**and**' to make one longer **sentence**, the sentence has a **capital letter** at the start and a **full stop** at the end.

The kite flew away and it landed in the tree.

More practice

1 Use the word '**and**' to join the two sentences. Write each new longer **sentence**.

Marie sat in the chair. She started to cry.

Marie sat in the chair and she started to cry.

The boy lay on his back. He looked at the clouds.

The boy lay on his back and he looked at the clouds.

Lucy saw a spider. She ran away.

Lucy saw a spider and she ran away.

2 Write a **sentence** about each picture.

The girl digs a hole.   She plants a tree.

Now join the two sentences together using '**and**'.

The girl digs a hole and she plants a tree.

Sentence practice

Write a sentence about <u>two</u> things you did this morning. Use the word '**and**'.

I got up and I brushed my teeth.

19

Check that the sentences are correctly punctuated with one capital letter at the start and one full stop at the end. There should be no capital letter for 'and' or the word after 'and'.

Accept answers where the pronoun has been omitted [e.g. Marie sat in the chair and started to cry.].

This is just an example of two shorter sentences and a possible longer sentence. Accept any sentences that make sense in relation to the pictures and are correctly punctuated with one capital letter and one full stop.

This is just an example of a sentence containing two activities joined by 'and'. Accept any sentence that makes sense and is correctly punctuated.

Lesson 7 More capital letters

Focus using capital letters for place names, days of the week and months of the year

Key terms word, capital letter

Focus text **On Saturday, Maisie went shopping in London.**
On Sunday, Maisie visited Aunt Lucy. She lives on Clifton Road.

TEACH

Display the focus text and read it aloud. Discuss where Maisie went on Saturday and Sunday. Then ask: How many capital letters are there in the first sentence? How many in the second and third? Underline all the words with capital letters. Discuss why these words need a special capital letter. Recap familiar uses of capital letters [the start of a sentence, a person's name, the word 'I'] and introduce new uses [place names, days of the week, months of the year].

Explain that place names, as well as people's names, always start with capital letters, even if they are in the middle of a sentence. This includes names of towns, streets, countries, continents and other places. Invite the children to name local towns or streets that would begin with capital letters.

Point out that sometimes people's names or place names are made up of two words [e.g. Aunt Lucy; Clifton Road]. Here both words start with a capital letter. Discuss other examples [e.g. Mrs Hills].

Explain that the days of the week [and months of the year] also always start with a capital letter. Look for these special words around the classroom [e.g. on calendars, reminders, displays].

ACTIVITY Play a game of 'Count the capitals' using the sentences from the photocopy master on the opposite page. Read a sentence aloud. Let the children count the words needing a capital letter, holding up the right number of fingers. Then show the sentence and discuss why each word needs a capital letter.

EXTEND Look at other uses of capital letters [e.g. names of subjects; titles of books].

PRACTISE

Pupil book pages 20–21

APPLY

- The children keep a diary for a week. They record events and activities in class [e.g. Today is Wednesday. We are going swimming with Mr Roberts.].
- Ask the children to write about their weekend [e.g. where they went and who they met]. Remind them to use capital letters for 'I' and the names of people, places and days.
- In other subjects, ask the children to keep a daily record [e.g. in science – to record the growth of seeds].
- The children write invitations to a party [e.g. linked to a story]. Focus on the use of capital letters for names, as well as the date and place of the party.
- In geography, remind children to use capital letters for place names [e.g. streets, towns, cities, countries and continents].
- The children draw maps of real or imaginary places [e.g. the local area; a pirate's treasure map] using capital letters for place names.

ASSESS

Dictation: Ella is going to Spain on Sunday.
Check: The sentence is correctly punctuated with three capital letters and a full stop.

Count the capital letters in each sentence. Which sentence has the most capital letters?

I think Jill Brown lives on Barnes Road in Leeds.

I will see my friend Scott on Saturday.

On Monday Mrs Jenkins got the coach to Oxford.

My dog Stanley is two today.

I sit next to Jessica Higgins.

I showed Mr Bell the map of France.

Cardiff is a city in Wales.

I go to the park with my friend.

My birthday is in the month of April.

Pupil book answers

More capital letters

Remember

Capital letters are used at the start of place names, as well as people's names.

Maisie went shopping in London.

Try it

1 Circle the **capital letter** at the start of any names you can see.

Ⓚate went to Ⓢpain for a week.

Ⓞmar took the bus to Ⓒhester.

Last week Ⓝur drove to Ⓦales.

We think Ⓗolly lives in Ⓟark Ⓛane.

Ⓛiz met Ⓜrs Ⓢcott on the corner of Ⓑright Ⓢtreet.

2 Copy the sentence and add the **capital letters** at the start of any names.

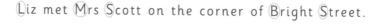

ross lives in manchester.	Ross lives in Manchester.
yasmin went to cardiff.	Yasmin went to Cardiff.
vishal has a map of liverpool.	Vishal has a map of Liverpool.
mr brown is in scotland.	Mr Brown is in Scotland.
adam ran down marsh lane.	Adam ran down Marsh Lane.

20

In the last two questions, check that both capital letters are circled in 'Park Lane', 'Mrs Scott' and 'Bright Street'.

The capital letters at the start of sentences should not be circled unless they are also names.

The capital letters should be the correct shape, the same height as any ascenders and taller than letters without ascenders.

In the last two questions, check that both words in 'Mr Brown' and 'Marsh Lane' are given capital letters.

Remember

The days of the week and the months of the year always start with a **capital letter**.

On Saturday, Maisie went shopping.

More practice

1 Look at Megan's calendar. Complete each sentence by adding the correct day of the week.

March

Monday	Swimming
Tuesday	
Wednesday	P.E. ☺
Thursday	Dentist
Friday	Jonas coming to visit ☺
Saturday Sunday	

Megan has the dentist on _____Thursday_____.

She goes swimming on _____Monday_____.

Jonas is coming on _____Friday_____.

Megan has P.E. on _____Wednesday_____.

The children should have completed the sentence using the day shown on the calendar. You could talk about calendars and the information shown on Megan's calendar before the children complete the sentences.

Again, capital letters should be the correct shape and height. The days of the week should be spelt correctly.

2 Complete these sentences by adding a place name, a day of the week or a month of the year.

Today it is _____Tuesday_____.

We do art on _____Thursday_____.

I live in _____Coventry_____.

On _____Saturday_____ we go shopping in _____Birmingham_____.

My birthday is in _____June_____.

The children should answer these questions with their own choices. The fourth question could be answered with the name of a particular shop, which should still have a capital letter.

Expect the days of the week to be spelt correctly.

Sentence practice

Write a sentence with a person's name and a place name in it.

I went to America to see Uncle Ted.

21

This is just an example of a sentence a child might write.

The sentence must be correctly punctuated with capital letters of the correct shape and height. Check that capital letters are not used in other words.

Lesson 8 Adding –s and –es

Focus forming plurals; understanding the effect of adding –s or –es to nouns

Key terms word, **singular**, **plural**

Focus text **One** dog **chased two** cats.
One frog **saw three** bats.
One fox **scared four** snakes.
One goat **ate five** cakes.

TEACH

Display the focus text and read it aloud. Discuss how many there are of each animal. Do the pupils notice the number pattern in the rhyme? Read it together using fingers to show the numbers.

Read aloud the highlighted words. Discuss what happens to the words at the end of the sentences to show there is more than one cat, bat, snake or cake. Draw a ring round the –s added to the end of these words.

Introduce the words 'singular' [meaning 'one' – like 'single'] and 'plural' [meaning 'more than one']. Explain that –s [or –es] is added to the word to show there is more than one. [Note: The children do not need to know the term 'noun' at this stage but you can use it if you wish.]

Identify the singular and plural words in the number rhyme. Then change the word 'One' so that the lines begin 'Two ... Three ... Four ... Five ...'. Discuss how the highlighted words now need to change. Add –s to make the words into plurals [e.g. Two dogs chased two cats.].

When you come to the third line, explain that –es is added when words end with –ch, –sh, –s, –x or –z, to make them easier to say [e.g. Four foxes ...].

ACTIVITY Provide the children with the word cards from the photocopy master on the opposite page. Ask them to sort the words into two piles: singular and plural. Then make the singular words into plurals by adding –s or –es.

EXTEND Discuss some common irregular plurals [e.g. feet, not foots; children, not childs].

PRACTISE

Pupil book pages 22–23

APPLY

- Together, write some more lines for the focus text, continuing the pattern, or choose another number rhyme as a model, using different singular and plural words.
- Challenge the children to write descriptions of animals in science [e.g. giving the number of legs and wings] or shapes in mathematics [e.g. giving the number of sides and corners].
- The children write labels or captions for pictures or displays of items [e.g. three sunflowers, five apples].
- The children write lists of items seen in different settings or activities [e.g. a bird survey – two blackbirds, a magpie; a traffic count – five cars, one bike, two buses].

ASSESS

Dictation: The dog ran after the <u>rabbits</u>.
Say: Underline the plural word. Change another word into a plural.
Check: The sentence begins with a capital letter and ends with a full stop.
Answer: dogs

Cut out the word cards. Sort the singular words and the plural words.

boat	beads
shark	stones
horse	toys
basket	ducks
star	vans
brick	kisses
torch	matches
glass	foxes

Pupil book answers

Adding –s and –es

Remember

You add **–s** to the end of a **word** to show there is more than one of something. This makes a **plural**. 'Plural' means more than one.

one dog   (singular)   two dogs   (plural)

Try it

1 Add –s to make each word into a **plural**.

pen s   pencil s   ruler s   desk s   book s

teacher s   crayon s   boy s   tray s   girl s

2 Look at the picture. For each object, write how many you can see. One has been done for you.

The children should count the items in the picture and write phrases giving the number of each item. An example is given to show what is required.

Check that –s is not added to the word 'teapot', as there is only one of these.

bowl   two bowls   spoon   six spoons

teapot   one teapot   cup   three cups

fork   five forks   plate   two plates

22

Remember

If a **word** ends in –ch, –sh, –s, –x or –z, add **–es** to make a **plural**.

one fox   (singular)   two foxes   (plural)

More practice

1 Add **–s** or **–es** to make each word into a **plural**. Write the plural word.

bag and box   ___bags___ and ___boxes___

brush and broom   ___brushes___ and ___brooms___

witch and wizard   ___witches___ and ___wizards___

skirt and dress   ___skirts___ and ___dresses___

tree and bush   ___trees___ and ___bushes___

> The plural words should be spelt correctly.
>
> Remind the children that –es can be heard as an 'iz' sound and an extra syllable or beat at the end of words [e.g. boxes].

2 Add **–s** or **–es** to make one word into a **plural**. Then write each sentence correctly.

This hen has six chick.   This hen has six chicks.

She gave me three wish.   She gave me three wishes.

Rabbits live in hutch.   Rabbits live in hutches.

I like fish and chip.   I like fish and chips.

We all clap our hand.   We all clap our hands.

> The plural words should be spelt correctly.
>
> Check that the children's sentences have capital letters and full stops.

Sentence practice

Write a sentence with the **plurals** of these <u>two</u> **words** in it.

car   bus

I saw lots of cars and buses in town.

23

This is just an example of a suitable sentence.

The plural words should be spelt correctly.

The sentence should have a capital letter and a full stop.

Lesson 9 Question marks

Focus recognising questions; using question marks to demarcate questions

Key terms sentence, **question**, **question mark**, full stop

Focus text **Where have you been?**
What did you see?
Who did you meet?

TEACH

Display the focus text. Read each sentence aloud using appropriate intonation. Discuss what is special about the sentences and how they are different from other sentences [e.g. they do not end with a full stop; they ask something; their purpose is to *get* information rather than *give* information].

Read the questions together using appropriate intonation. In colour, write over each question mark as you reach it. Ask the children to write a question mark in the air as you do this.

Explain that these sentences are questions. Questions are sentences that ask something rather than tell something. Questions end with a question mark rather than a full stop. The question mark is important because it tells the reader to read the question with a 'question voice'.

Ask the children to read each question from the focus text using a 'question voice'. In the role of a character from a story [e.g. Jack and the Beanstalk], answer the questions using a complete sentence [e.g. I have been to the top of the beanstalk.]. Discuss the differences between the questions and the answers [e.g. 'asking' sentences and 'telling' sentences].

ACTIVITY Read aloud sentences from the photocopy master on the opposite page. Ask the children to shout 'question mark' and write a question mark in the air whenever they hear a question. Discuss how they know [e.g. the inflection in the voice; the 'question words' such as what, when, how].

EXTEND Discuss different types of question starter [e.g. Did you …? Can you …? Have you …?]. Discuss how these use the same intonation and are still asking something.

PRACTISE

Pupil book pages 24–25

APPLY

- Together, use questions like those in the focus text to question another story character [e.g. Little Red Riding Hood].
- Look for questions in stories and read them aloud appropriately. Ask the children to write speech bubbles for story characters containing the questions [e.g. Who's been sleeping in my bed?].
- The children read or make lift-the-flap books using repeated questions [e.g. Is Spot in the …? Where is my hat? Who is in the shed? What can you see?].
- Use a question hand [a cut-out hand shape with the words 'where', 'when', 'what', 'why', 'who' on each finger and 'how' on the palm] to prompt the children to ask questions in a range of subjects.
- Write questions to go on a display [e.g. How many coins?]. Write the question marks in colour.
- The children question a partner about an event. They take turns, with the questioner holding up a question mark.

ASSESS

Dictation: I can see you. Can you see me?
Check: Both sentences start with capital letters and end with the correct punctuation mark.

Cut out the sentences. Which of the sentences need a question mark?
Sort the sentences into 'Questions' and 'Not questions'.

I went to the lake

How did you get home

When did you get here

I was late

Why did you come

I found a box

What will you do now

I met the king

Did you see someone

Pupil book answers

Question marks

Remember

A sentence that asks something is called a **question**.
A question ends with a **question mark**.

Where have you been?
What did you see?
Who did you meet?

Try it

1 Read each question. Put a **question mark** at the end of it.

Where did you go ?
Who did you meet ?
How did you feel ?
Why did you go out ?
When did you get back ?
Did you feel sad ?

2 Put the words in order so they make a **question**. Write each question with a **question mark** at the end.

Check that the sentences also begin with a capital letter.

hid box the Who	Who hid the box?
is Where hat my	Where is my hat?
the bus come When will	When will the bus come?
can What you see	What can you see?
the ship How sink did	How did the ship sink?

24

48

Remember

All **sentences** start with a **capital letter**. Most sentences end with a **full stop**. **Questions** end with a **question mark**.

More practice

1 Read each sentence. Put a **full stop** or a **question mark** at the end.

Why did that happen__?__   It was cold in the garden__.__

We went to the coast__.__   Can you swim__?__

What did you do at school__?__   There is a frog in the pond__.__

2 Write <u>four</u> **questions** to ask the man in the picture.

What _happened?_

Why _are you running?_

Where _is the dog?_

Did the dog run away?

These are just examples of the sort of questions the children might write. Any question is acceptable as long as it makes sense in relation to the picture and ends with a question mark. [The last question should also start with a capital letter. It could begin with another question word or a question starter such as 'Did ...?']

Sentence practice

There is a new child in your class. Write a **question** to ask him or her.

What is your name?

25

This is an example of the sort of question the children might write. Any question is acceptable as long as it makes sense, starts with a capital letter and ends with a question mark.

Questions can start with question words or with question starters such as 'Have you ...?'; 'Can you ...?' Question words [e.g. what, who, why, when and where] should be spelt correctly as they all appear on these pages.

Lesson 10 Verb endings

Focus introducing verbs; adding endings such as –ed, –ing, –er to verbs

Key terms word, letter, **word ending**, **doing word** or **verb**

Focus text Banjo Bill likes to play the banjo. He likes playing happy tunes.
He plays for hours. Once he played all day and all night.
Banjo Bill is a great banjo player.

TEACH

Show the focus text and read it aloud. Discuss what Banjo Bill likes doing and what he once did.

Focus on the highlighted words. Ask the children what they notice about these words [e.g. they all contain the word 'play'; they have different endings]. Circle the different endings on the word 'play'.

Explain that the word 'play' is a 'doing' or action word – it tells us what Bill is doing. 'Doing words' are called 'verbs'. Verbs are very important because they tell us what is happening or what someone is doing. Discuss some other actions Bill might do [e.g. sing; think; smile; strum his banjo]. Invite the pupils to mime these actions. Endings such as –ing, –s and –ed are added on to verbs so that they can be used in different ways. Some sentences in the focus text would not make sense without the endings. Show this by reading aloud some of the sentences without the word endings [e.g. 'He likes play happy tunes.' needs the –ing ending; 'Once he play all day.' needs the –ed ending because it happened in the past].

Discuss how adding –er changes the word completely. Rather than naming an action [play] it names someone who does that action [a player]. Discuss other examples [e.g. paint/painter; sing/singer].

Rework the focus text using a different verb [e.g. paint]. Ask the children to supply the words with endings [e.g. Bonnie Brush likes to paint. She likes painting bright pictures. She is a good painter.].

ACTIVITY Choose a verb from the photocopy master on the opposite page and ask the children to find all the endings that can be added to it. Discuss what is/is not a word [e.g. standing, stands, but not standed, stander]. Point out that adding –er sometimes makes the name of a *thing* that does the action, rather than a person [e.g. cooker].

EXTEND Explore further the use of the –ed ending, to show actions that happened in the past. [Note: The past and present tenses are covered in more detail in **Grammar 2.**]

PRACTISE

Pupil book pages 26–27

APPLY

- List –er words that name people and ask the children to make up appropriate names [e.g. Banjo Bill, the banjo player; Mr Tick, the teacher; Bobby Bucket, the cleaner].
- The children write captions for pictures, using verbs with –ing endings [e.g. Beth is feeding the hens.].
- When reading stories together, look for verbs with –ed endings [e.g. Jenny splashed in the puddle.].
- Help the children to use the correct word endings when writing sentences or accounts of events.
- Play games where some of the children mime verbs and others ask questions [e.g. Are you singing? Are you a singer?].

ASSESS

Dictation: Mum needed the toaster. Dad was fixing it.
Say: Underline the words with added endings.
Check: The underlined words are spelt correctly.

Cut out the verbs.

jump	buzz	cook
wait	bump	hunt
start	read	add
dream	stand	limp
melt	bark	fall
pick	turn	climb

Cut out the word endings. Which of these endings can you add to each of the verbs?

–ing	–ed	–s	–er

Pupil book answers

Verb endings

Remember

Some words tell you what people are doing. '**Doing words**' are also called **verbs**. You can add the **word endings –ing, –ed, –s** and **–er** on to the end of verbs.

play   play**ing**   play**ed**   play**s**   play**er**

Try it

The words should be spelt correctly.

1 Add the **endings** to the end of these verbs. Write each new **word**.

clean + ing = ___cleaning___   clean + er = ___cleaner___

sing + er = ___singer___   sing + ing = ___singing___

push + ing = ___pushing___   push + ed = ___pushed___

wait + ed = ___waited___   wait + er = ___waiter___

float + s = ___floats___   float + ing = ___floating___

Check that the children have underlined two words in each sentence.

You could discuss which words are verbs that describe the person's actions, and which words *name* someone who does something [e.g. painter, player, starter].

2 Underline each **word** with the ending **–ed, –ing, –s** or **–er**.

The <u>painter</u> <u>painted</u> the door red.

Jenny <u>helps</u> with <u>washing</u> the car.

Mum is <u>cooking</u> stew and I am <u>watching</u>.

The football <u>player</u> <u>played</u> his best game.

She <u>looked</u> at the frog and <u>sighed</u>.

The <u>starter</u> <u>starts</u> the race.

26

Remember

You can use **verbs** in different ways when you add **word endings** to them.

The banjo player likes playing the banjo.

More practice

1 Add the **endings –er** and **–ing** so the sentences make sense.

Zack was play ing on his scoot er .

The sing er likes sing ing sad songs.

Dad put the fry ing pan on the cook er .

The road sweep er is sweep ing up the rubbish.

2 Look at the picture. Complete the **sentences** to say what everyone is doing. Use words with the **ending –ing**.

4+6=

Alex

Lucas   Poppy

Alex is thinking.

Lucas is reading.

Poppy is counting.

The teacher is writing on the whiteboard.

These are just example sentences using words ending with –ing. The sentence should say what the children are doing in the picture. You could talk about the events in the picture before the children write the sentences.

Check that the sentences end with full stops.

Sentence practice

Add the **endings –ing** and **–er** to the word '**print**'. Then use the two new **words** in a sentence.

I am printing my work on the printer.

27

This is just an example sentence using the words 'printer' and 'printing'.

Check that the sentence starts with a capital letter and ends with a full stop.

Revision 2 answers

These pages revise concepts introduced in Sections 1 and 2. The focus of each activity is given to help identify areas where the children might need further revision.

Grammar 1   Schofield & Sims **Grammar and Punctuation**

Revision 2

Focus: using full stops and question marks to demarcate sentences

1 Something is missing from the end of each **sentence**. Write it in.

Where is the car_?_

The van went up the hill__.

When will you get home_?_

I get the bus to school__.

Did you see a blue truck_?_

A bike has two wheels__.

Focus: combining words to make sentences; using 'and' to join words

Use this activity to remind the children about the importance of rereading sentences to check that they make sense and to look for missing words.

The third sentence could have other words instead of 'at' [e.g. 'for'; 'in'].

2 There is a missing **word** in each **sentence**. Write the sentence correctly.

We saw the cows sheep.

We saw the cows and sheep.

They sang for the king queen.

They sang for the king and queen.

I like looking books.

I like looking at books.

Focus: using 'and' to join sentences

Check that the answer is correctly punctuated as one sentence [i.e. no full stops or capital letters within the sentence].

Accept answers where 'she' is missed out.

3 Read the start of the story. Put in the missing **capital letters** and **full stops**.

O   S
once there was a girl called Ruby . she had lots of money .

4 Write these two sentences as **one** **sentence** using the word '**and**'.

Mum broke a cup. She was sad.

Mum broke a cup and she was sad.

28

Focus: using capital letters and full stops to demarcate sentences

The children need to identify that there are <u>two</u> sentences here. They may just add a capital letter at the start and a full stop at the end. Look for the full stop at the end of the first sentence and the capital letter at the start of the second.

The children may have difficulty identifying the sentence boundaries. If so, encourage them to read the sentences aloud so they can hear the sentence breaks. They should use the same technique when checking their own writing.

5 Underline <u>two</u> **words** in the sentence that need to start with a **capital letter**. Then write the words correctly.

We saw <u>ella</u> and <u>alfie</u> on the beach.

   Ella   Alfie   •

Mr <u>jones</u> took us to <u>belfast</u>.

   Jones   Belfast

On <u>monday</u> <u>i</u> went to town.

   Monday   I

In <u>march</u> I will go to <u>italy</u>.

   March   Italy

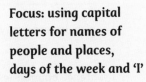

Focus: using capital letters for names of people and places, days of the week and 'I'

The capital letters at the start of sentences should not be underlined as they already start with capital letters.

Check that the capital letters at the start of the words are of the correct shape and size compared to other letters.

6 Look at the picture. Write how many of each object you can see. One has been done for you.

mask	three masks	button	six buttons
bead	ten beads	brush	five brushes
card	two cards	crayon	seven crayons

29

Focus: adding –s and –es to make plurals

The children should follow the example given and write phrases giving the number of each item as shown in the picture.

The plural nouns should be spelt correctly. [It does not matter if the children have miscounted the items.]

Writing task 2: Analysis sheet

Tick the circles to show amount of evidence found in writing:

1 No evidence
2 Some evidence
3 Clear evidence

Pupil name: _____

Date: _____

Assessing punctuation

The writing sample demonstrates:	Evidence		
capital letters used at the beginning of sentences.	①	②	③
sentence boundaries recognised and demarcated with full stops.	①	②	③
question marks used to demarcate questions [e.g. Can you come?].	①	②	③
capital letters used for 'I', names of people and places, days of the week and the months of the year.	①	②	③
capital letters used only where needed – no incorrect use [e.g. in the middle of words or sentences].	①	②	③

Assessing grammar and sentence structure

The writing sample demonstrates:	Evidence		
words formed into complete sentences [e.g. I am having a party. It is on Saturday.].	①	②	③
grammatically correct sentences [e.g. no missing words].	①	②	③
appropriate spacing between words.	①	②	③
the word 'and' used to join some words and clauses [e.g. We will dress up and play games.].	①	②	③

Key target: _____

Writing task 2: Pupil checklist

Name: _____   Date: _____

Reread what you have written to check that it makes sense. Tick the circle if you have correctly used the punctuation or grammar feature in your writing.

Punctuation

◯ I have used capital letters at the beginning of sentences.

◯ I have used full stops at the end of sentences.

◯ I have used question marks at the end of questions.

◯ I have used capital letters for 'I', names, the days of the week and the months of the year.

Grammar and sentences

◯ I have said my sentences aloud before writing them.

◯ I have checked that my sentences make sense and are complete.

◯ I have left spaces between my words.

◯ I have used the word 'and' to join words and to make a longer sentence.

Teacher feedback

My key target: _____

_____

Lesson 11 Exclamation marks

Focus   introducing exclamation marks at the end of sentences

Key terms   sentence, **exclamation mark**, full stop, question mark, capital letter

Focus text   The gingerbread man jumped out of the oven.

> Well, I never!   Don't eat me!   Stop!   Come back at once!

TEACH

Display the focus text and read the opening sentence. Ask: Do you recognise the story? Talk about the characters and what happens. Read the words in the speech bubbles and discuss who might be speaking. Then discuss *how* the characters might speak these lines [e.g. with surprise; loudly; with anger]. Read the speech bubbles together using appropriate expression.

Point out the exclamation mark at the end of these sentences. Write over the exclamation marks in a different colour. Ask the children to write exclamation marks in the air. Use an appropriate 'surprising' sound effect to accompany the writing action.

Explain that an exclamation mark is used rather than a full stop to show that a sentence needs to be read with feeling. The exclamation mark gives a message to the reader. For example, it tells us to read a sentence loudly, or with surprise, anger, fear or excitement.

The focus text shows that many sentences with exclamation marks are shorter than normal sentences [e.g. Stop!]. Point out that a capital letter is still needed at the start, even if the sentence is only one word.

Read aloud the opening sentence of the focus text [which ends with a full stop]. Explain that you *could* change the full stop to an exclamation mark – but only because the sentence tells us something particularly surprising. Make the change and read it aloud with appropriate expression.

ACTIVITY   Give the children punctuation paddles from the photocopy master on the opposite page. Say sentences aloud and ask the children to hold up the correct punctuation mark. Discuss how they know [e.g. by the intonation; by what it says or asks].

EXTEND   Look at different types of sentence that end with an exclamation mark [e.g. ordinary sentences that tell us something surprising; short interjections such as 'Ow!'].

PRACTISE

Pupil book pages 32–33

APPLY

- Together, look for exclamation marks while reading. Discuss why they are used and read the sentences aloud with appropriate expression.
- Collect and display lots of different examples of sentences with exclamation marks. Write the exclamation marks in bright colours.
- The children write the story of The Gingerbread Man, using some exclamations.
- The children write speech bubbles for characters from other stories, using exclamation marks to show different feelings [e.g. Oh no!; I won!].

ASSESS

Dictation: Go away! I will not speak to you.

Say: End one of these sentences with an exclamation mark. Decide which one would be best.

Check: The other sentence ends with a full stop.

Cut out the punctuation paddles and stick them on to card.

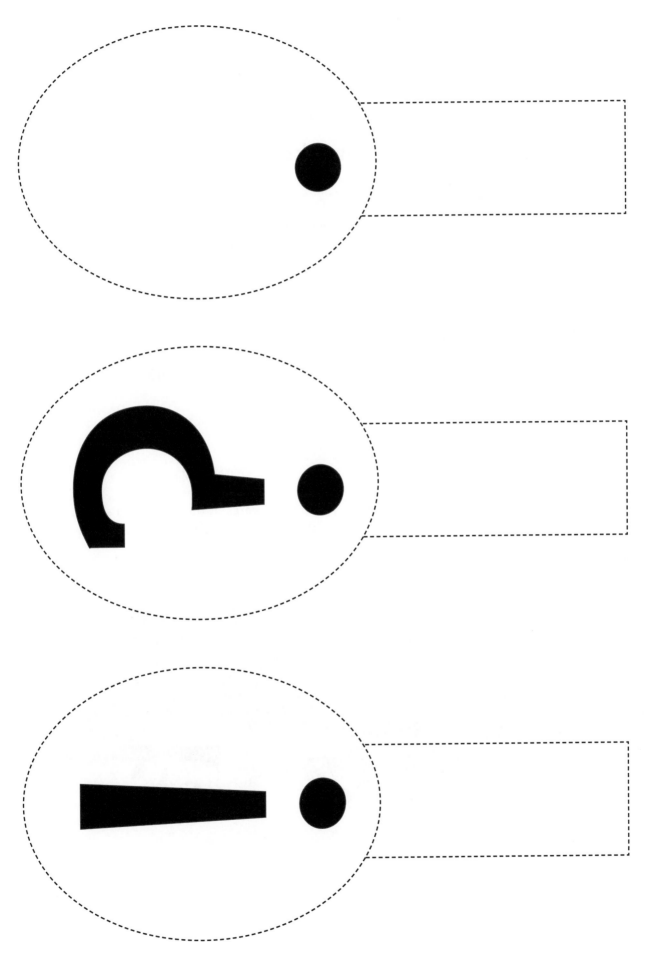

Pupil book answers

Exclamation marks

Remember

Some sentences end with an **exclamation mark**. The exclamation mark tells you to read the sentence with strong feeling or in a loud voice.

Don't eat me!   Stop!   Come back at once!

Listen to the children reading the sentences aloud to check that they use appropriate expression. Discuss what expression is needed for each sentence.

Try it

1. Put an **exclamation mark** at the end of the sentence. Then read it aloud with feeling.

Wait for me__!__   I want my mummy__!__

You are so funny__!__   I'm six today__!__

Leave me alone__!__   Don't be silly__!__

The children should select suitable words to show the feelings of the characters or their situation. You could discuss the events and the feelings of the characters with the children before they begin the exercise.

The words should start with capital letters and be followed by an exclamation mark.

2. Look at the picture. Write these words in the bubbles to show the different feelings. Remember to use an **exclamation mark**.

Splash   Help   Shoo   Oops   Boo

32

60

Remember

Most sentences end with a **full stop**.
Only use an **exclamation mark** if the
sentence tells the reader something
surprising or exciting.

The gingerbread man jumped out of the oven!

More practice

1 Read the sentences. Put an **exclamation mark** at the end of
three sentences. End the other two sentences with a **full stop**.

The grass was made of jelly__!__

I am going home__.__

Bob fell in the pond__!__

The man walked down the path__.__

We found an elephant in the garden__!__

Discuss why the
children chose to end
those three sentences
with an exclamation
mark [e.g. What
surprising or exciting
thing does each one
tell us?].

2 Put the words in order so that they make a sentence that can
end with an **exclamation mark**.

my It is today birthday   It is my birthday today!

I a you surprise for have   I have a surprise for you!

there right Stop   Stop right there!

went The pop balloon   The balloon went pop!

Check that the
sentences also start
with capital letters.

Sentence practice

Complete this sentence so that it ends with an **exclamation
mark**.

You are _the winner!_

33

This is one example – the children may have
chosen other endings [e.g. You are great!].

Lesson 12 Writing in sentences

> Focus breaking ideas into a sequence of separate sentences demarcated by capital letters and full stops
>
> Key terms sentence, word, capital letter, full stop, **punctuation**, **punctuation mark**
>
> Focus text **Jamie went on holiday. He went camping with his family. They played on the beach and swam in the sea.**

TEACH

Do not show the focus text but read it aloud. Ask: How many sentences are there? [three] Read the text again with the children showing their hands to indicate the end of a sentence. Discuss how they know it is the end of a sentence [e.g. you hear the pause; the idea is complete].

Show the text. Underline each sentence in a different colour. Circle the three full stops and capital letters. Discuss what each sentence tells us. Which sentence tells us two things? [the one with 'and']

Explain that when we write, we break our ideas up into a series of sentences. If Jamie were here *telling* us about his holiday, he might say 'I went on holiday *and* we went camping *and* we played on the beach and swam in the sea *and* ...', but in writing, we break ideas into separate sentences, with each sentence telling us one complete idea [or two if we use 'and'].

Remind the children that all sentences begin with a capital letter and end with a full stop, unless they are special sentences that need a question mark or an exclamation mark. Explain that this is called sentence punctuation and it is a way of separating our sentences to make our writing clearer. Explain that full stops, question marks and exclamation marks can also be called punctuation marks.

Jointly compose three sentences about another event [e.g. Jamie's party]. Write each sentence in a different colour [e.g. Jamie is having ...; He is going to ...; His friends will ...]. Involve the children in the process of saying each sentence, writing and punctuating it, and then reading and checking it.

ACTIVITY In pairs, ask the children to orally compose three sentences about one of the pictures from the photocopy master on the opposite page.

EXTEND Build up the number of sentences you ask the children to compose and write.

PRACTISE

Pupil book pages 34–35

APPLY

- Ask the children to write a given number of sentences on a topic or theme [e.g. to describe a plant in science or a famous person in history].
- The children write accounts of events [e.g. going on a trip], composing sentences to answer different questions [e.g. Where did you go? Who with? What did you do?].
- Use story circles to practise retelling familiar stories in sentences. Tell the story round the circle, with each child adding a sentence at a time. Hold up full-stop paddles at the end of the sentence.
- The children use writing partners to orally rehearse a sequence of sentences before writing them.
- Always remind the children to punctuate each sentence as they write it. Make this a key target.

ASSESS

Dictation: The dog barked at the cat. The cat ran away and hid in a tree. The dog barked at the tree.
Check: The three sentences are correctly punctuated with capital letters and full stops.

Cut out the pictures. Choose a picture. Make up <u>three</u> sentences about where Jamie went and what he did.

Pupil book answers

Writing in sentences

Remember

When you write, you break your ideas up into a number of **sentences**. Each sentence starts with a **capital letter** and ends with a **full stop**.

Jamie went on holiday. He went camping with his family. They played on the beach and swam in the sea.

Try it

1 Read the two sentences on each line. Then add a **sentence** of your own.

It rained all day on Monday. The children had to stay inside.

  They were bored.

Bill was in a rowing boat. The boat started to fill with water.

  Bill shouted for help.

Alice went to the beach. She went for a swim in the sea.

  She saw a jellyfish and ran back to the beach.

I saw a frog in the long grass. It was green with big eyes.

  It jumped in the pond and swam away.

2 Here are <u>three</u> **sentences**. They have no **capital letters** or **full stops**. Write them correctly.

the boy had a toy car he pushed it down the hill it went fast and crashed into a tree

  The boy had a toy car. He pushed it down the hill. It went fast

  and crashed into a tree.

These are examples of sentences the children might add. The sentences should be correctly punctuated and related to the theme of the first two sentences.

The first two examples are short simple sentences; the second two show sentences using 'and'. You could prompt the children to use 'and' in at least one of their sentences.

34

Check that the children correctly identify the sentence boundaries. Reading the sentences aloud will help them hear the sentence breaks. This is an important skill, as although children are encouraged to put in sentence punctuation as they write, young learners are likely to forget. They must also learn to reread, listening for sentence breaks and putting punctuation in place.

Some of the children may put a full stop after 'fast'. If so, point out that the sentence continues with 'and' so it is not the end of the sentence.

Remember

Say your sentence. Write it. Then read it. Check that it makes sense and has the correct **punctuation**.

More practice

1 Read these three **sentences** carefully. Check that they make sense. Write them correctly.

Mum put the cake the oven. She went outside water the plants. She forgot about the cake it burnt.

Mum put the cake in the oven. She went outside to water the

plants. She forgot about the cake and it burnt.

The children may have corrected the sentences in different ways that are still correct [e.g. She went outside and watered the plants. She forgot about the cake. It burnt.].

2 Write <u>three</u> **sentences** about the picture. Say each sentence, write it and then check it.

The girl is painting a picture.

She drops a pot of paint on the floor.

It makes a mess and she is sad.

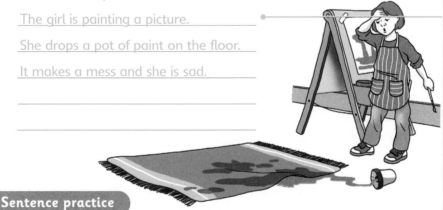

This is an example of three related sentences about the event shown in the picture. There should be three clear sentences, each starting with a capital letter and ending with a full stop.

See if the children include a sentence using 'and'. If not, you could discuss possibilities.

Sentence practice

Write <u>three</u> sentences about finding a caterpillar.

I found a caterpillar in the garden. I saw it crawling on a leaf.

It was green and hairy.

35

This is an example of three related sentences about the given event. Each sentence should start with a capital letter and end with a full stop.

Look to see if the children include a sentence using 'and'. If not, you could ask them to do this [e.g. orally extending one of their sentences].

Lesson 13 Linking sentences

Focus sequencing sentences to form short narratives or accounts

Key terms sentence, **linking word**

Focus text **The little goat ran away from the farmyard and he saw the farm cat sleeping by the gate and he saw three ducks quacking.**

TEACH

Show the focus text and read it aloud as it is written, without any pauses. Ask: What is wrong with this story? [e.g. it keeps using 'and'; it is not in separate sentences; it sounds more like how we speak than how we write]

Read the focus text again, pausing at the end of each shorter sentence. Cross out the word 'and' and put in a full stop and capital letter. Read the new version of the text. Ask how else it could be improved.

Explain that the focus text tells us about a series of events that follow on from each other. We can use special words at the start of sentences like these to show the sequence of events or the order in which things happen [e.g. what happened *first, then* what happened …]. These words are called 'linking words'.

Demonstrate adding the word 'First' to the start of the second sentence of the focus text and 'Then' to the start of the third sentence. Read the new version of the text together.

Invite the children to compose a sentence to say what happened *next*. Start with the word 'Next'.

ACTIVITY In pairs, ask the children to use the story map and the linking words included in the photocopy master on the opposite page to tell the complete story of where the little goat went.

EXTEND Discuss other linking words and when to use the different words [e.g. 'First' is used for the first event; 'Finally' for the last; 'Suddenly' or 'Soon' for something that happens quickly].

PRACTISE

Pupil book pages 36–37

APPLY

- The children write their own story of the little goat with different characters and events. They use a linking word for each new event or character he meets.
- The children write personal accounts of a sequence of events at school or home [e.g. sports day; a school trip; a day out] using linking words.
- Look for linking words when reading different texts. Collect and display these words as models.
- Ask the children to highlight linking words they use in their own writing.
- In other areas of the curriculum [e.g. history], find opportunities for the children to order pictures to show a sequence of events. They then write sentences to go with the pictures using linking words to form an account of the events.
- In science, challenge the children to write a sequence of sentences [e.g. to describe how plants change over time] using linking words.

ASSESS

Dictation: First I ate my toast.
Say: Write a sentence to say what you did next. Use a linking word.
Check: A linking word is used and the sentence has a capital letter and a full stop.
Answer: e.g. Then I drank my milk.

Use the story map and the linking words to tell the story of what happened to the little goat.

The little goat ran away from the farmyard ...

Finally ...

First ...

Then ...

So then ...

Next ...

Suddenly ...

Pupil book answers

Linking sentences

Remember

Sometimes you write sentences about a series of events. Start the sentences with **linking words** to show the order of events.

The little goat ran away from the farmyard. First he saw the farm cat sleeping by the gate. Then he saw three ducks quacking.

Try it

1 Underline any **linking words** at the start of a sentence.

Dad washed the car. <u>Later</u> he drove to town.

Hayden put on his coat. <u>Then</u> he put on his hat and scarf.

Kelly found some leaves. <u>Next</u> she found some seeds.

Isabelle went to bed. <u>Soon</u> she was fast asleep.

Jake was playing. <u>Suddenly</u> a big dog barked at him.

2 Add a **linking word** to start the second sentence on each line.

I went on the swings. _____Then_____ I went on the slide.

Oliver went into the woods. _____Soon_____ he was lost.

Sunil was digging a hole. _____Suddenly_____ she found a gold coin.

Simeon had a wash. _____Next_____ he brushed his teeth.

We played on the beach all morning. _____Later_____ we went in the sea.

Often another word will work just as well [e.g. I went on the swings. <u>Next</u> I went on the slide.]. Discuss alternatives with the children.

The added word must start with a capital letter as it is at the start of the sentence.

36

Schofield & Sims **Grammar and Punctuation**   Grammar 1

> ### Remember
> You can use **linking words** to help you write stories or to write about things that happen.

More practice

1 Write the missing **sentences** to say what happened. Start your sentences with a **linking word**.

1.

We went for a picnic.

2.

Soon it began to rain.

3.

We stood under a tree.

4.

Later the sun came out
and we had our picnic.

2 Complete the **sentences** to say what the children did at the zoo.

First the children saw the tigers.

Then they saw the lions.

Next they saw the monkeys.

Finally they went home.

Sentence practice

Write the next <u>two</u> sentences to say what happened. Start both your sentences with a **linking word**.

We went to the shops. First we went to the bakers to get some bread. Then we went to the toy shop.

37

These are examples of sentences beginning with appropriate words. The sentences should describe the events shown in the pictures to form a sequence of linked sentences.

The sentences should be correctly punctuated.

These are examples of sentences giving a suitable sequence of linked events. The children may have written longer sentences using 'and'. You could discuss this with the children [e.g. First they saw the tigers and they were big.].

Check that the sentences all end with full stops.

These are examples of sentences giving a sequence of related events. Again, the children may have written longer sentences using 'and'.

Check that both sentences are correctly punctuated.

Lesson 14 Describing words

Focus using describing words to add detail to a sentence

Key terms sentence, **describing word**

Focus text The hen met a fox.
The little hen met a big fox.
The little brown hen met a thin red fox.

TEACH

Reveal the focus text a sentence at a time. Discuss the extra details added to the second and third sentences [the size and colour of the hen and the fox]. Underline the added words [little, big, brown, thin, red]. Discuss why these words make the sentence more interesting [e.g. a 'big' fox might be more of a danger; a 'thin' fox might be a hungry fox].

Explain that we add extra 'describing words' into a sentence to add more detail and make our sentences more interesting. Describing words like 'big', 'little', 'thin', 'brown', 'red' [which describe size and colour] help to create a picture in our heads – but describing words can also give other important details [e.g. 'thin' makes us think the fox might be in need of a meal]. [Note: The children do not need to know the term 'adjective' at this stage, but you can use it if you wish.]

Discuss other words that might be used to describe the fox [e.g. fat; hungry; fast; sleek; clever; cunning; sad]. Demonstrate how to try out these words in the original sentence, saying the new sentence aloud to see which words sound best or make the most interesting sentence [e.g. The little brown hen met a cunning red fox/a sad thin fox.].

ACTIVITY Read a sentence from the photocopy master on the opposite page. Discuss where describing words could be added to extend the sentence and make it more detailed. Ask the children to work in pairs and discuss possible words, trying them out in the sentence. Listen to different versions of the sentence, discussing the extra words that have been chosen. What extra details do they add? [e.g. size; colour; qualities]

EXTEND Discuss other ways of adding extra detail into a sentence [e.g. The giant lived in a castle on the hill near a forest.].

PRACTISE

Pupil book pages 38–39

APPLY

- When orally rehearsing sentences for stories or accounts, prompt the children to add more detail by choosing extra words to add to the sentence [e.g. What colour was it? What did it look like?].
- Provide sentence stems to encourage the use of describing words to create interesting pictures [e.g. I opened the door and saw a ...].
- Together, make lists of describing words used in other subjects [e.g. to describe size in mathematics – long, short, tall; materials in science – shiny, dull, soft, hard]. Display these in the classroom.
- When reading stories and poems, look for interesting describing words. Use sentences from stories as models for pupils to create their own sentences with describing words.

ASSESS

Dictation: The fast car was next to a bus.
Say: Underline the describing word. Add another describing word into the sentence.
Check: An adjective has been added. The sentence is punctuated correctly.
Answer: e.g. The fast car was next to a slow bus.

Choose a sentence. Add one or more describing words to the sentence.

She picked a flower from the garden.

The giant lived in a castle.

The lady baked a pie.

The van went up the hill.

The princess lived in a tower.

The dog had spots.

The man had a suitcase.

We saw stars in the sky.

Pupil book answers

Describing words

Remember

You can add **describing words** to a sentence to give more detail.

The hen met a fox.

The little hen met a big fox.

Try it

1 Underline the **describing word** in each sentence.

I put on my green shorts.

There was a big spider in the bath.

Rose found a magic shell.

Leo is wearing a fluffy jumper.

I need a cold drink.

These are examples of suitable words but the children may have made different choices.

Discuss the choices made. Which give the best detail? Which of them describe colour? What else do they describe?

2 Add a **describing word** to each sentence to give more detail.

I like _____juicy_____ apples best.

Lizzy found a _____silver_____ coin.

The moth had _____brown_____ wings.

I like a _____soft_____ pillow to sleep on.

We saw the _____angry_____ bull in the field.

Cinderella had two _____nasty_____ sisters.

38

Schofield & Sims **Grammar and Punctuation**   Grammar 1

Remember

You can use two **describing words** together to make your sentences more interesting.

The hen met a fox.
The little brown hen met a thin red fox.

More practice

1 Write each sentence with <u>two</u> extra **describing words**.

The kitten was stuck in a tree.

The little kitten was stuck in a tall tree.

A girl ran into the woods.

A young girl ran into the dark woods.

Again, these are examples of words that could be used. Discuss the different choices made. Do they make interesting sentences?

The children could use a pair of describing words rather than two separate words [e.g. A girl ran into the deep dark woods.].

2 Look at the picture. Write <u>three</u> **sentences** about what the girl is wearing. Use all of the **describing words** below.

warm   thick   long   woolly   black   smart

The girl is wearing a thick jacket and warm mittens.

She has a long scarf and a woolly hat.

She has smart black boots.

These are examples of sentences the children might write. Discuss their choices of describing words to go with the picture.

This activity also provides a good opportunity for writing sentences using 'and'.

Check that the three sentences start with capital letters and end with full stops.

Sentence practice

Write a sentence about a mouse. Use <u>two</u> **describing words** in your sentence.

The little brown mouse ran away.

39

This is just one example of a sentence using two words to describe the mouse. The children might use two separate words [e.g. The brown mouse lived in a little hole.].

Discuss different choices. Which give the best detail?

Lesson 15 Adding un–

Focus understanding how the prefix un– changes the meaning of words [adjectives and verbs]

Key terms word, doing word or verb, describing word

Focus text **Bruno the bear was happy. He was a very lucky bear.**
Barney the bear was unhappy. He was a very unlucky bear.

TEACH

Show the first two sentences of the focus text and read them aloud. What do they tell us about Bruno the bear? Underline the words that describe Bruno [happy, lucky].

Reveal the rest of the text and read it aloud. What does it tell us about Barney? Underline the words 'unhappy', 'unlucky'. Discuss what the children notice about the underlined words [e.g. un– is added to the start of words; the words have opposite meanings]. Ask the children to make happy and unhappy faces.

Explain that un– is added to the start of a describing word to change its meaning. Un– means 'not', so it makes a word that means the opposite ['unhappy' is 'not happy'; 'unlucky' is 'not lucky']. [Note: Un– is a prefix. The children do not need to know the term yet, but you can introduce it if you wish.]

Discuss other pairs of words like this. Say some more describing words [e.g. kind; fit] and ask the children to say the opposite by adding un–. Act out the different meanings [e.g. a fit person and an unfit person].

Explain that un– is sometimes added to doing words, or verbs [e.g. I tie my laces. Then I untie them.]. Mime these actions with the children. Establish that adding un– means 'undoing' the action.

ACTIVITY Ask two of the children to choose a verb from the photocopy master on the opposite page. Let them mime the word without and then with un– [e.g. one child does up his buttons; the other undoes them]. Let the other children guess the verbs.

EXTEND Discuss words that can/cannot be reversed by adding un– [e.g. Can we say 'unbig', 'unhungry'? Is 'unbreak' a word?].

PRACTISE

Pupil book pages 40–41

APPLY

- When reading, encourage the children to look for words with un– . They then record them with pictures to show their meaning.
- The children write pairs of sentences using words with un– [e.g. ... makes me happy; ... makes me unhappy. I am afraid of ...; I am unafraid of ...].
- The children draw pictures and write sentences or character profiles about two opposite characters [e.g. Mr Kind and Mr Unkind; Miss Tidy and Miss Untidy].
- In activities [e.g. making things in design and technology], use verbs and adjectives with the un– prefix [e.g. fold/unfold, do/undo, pick/unpick; Is your tower safe or unsafe?].

ASSESS

Dictation: I dress in the morning and I <u>undress</u> at night.
Say: Underline the word starting with un–.
Check: The word 'undress' is spelt correctly. The sentence is correctly punctuated.

Cut up the word cards. Add un– to the verbs to make new words.

do	tie	fold
load	dress	zip
lock	pack	wind
roll	screw	hook
cover	fasten	curl

un	un	un	un	un
un	un	un	un	un
un	un	un	un	un

Pupil book answers

Adding un–

Remember

If you add the letters **un–** to the start of a **describing word** it makes a word that means the opposite.

lucky   unlucky

Try it

1. Add **un–** to the **describing word** to make a word that means the opposite.

   Tilly was ____un kind to me.   The rules are ____un fair.

   The story was ____un true.   The king was ____un wise to trust you.

2. Add **un–** to the **describing word** to make a word that matches the next picture.

happy   tidy   fit

unhappy   untidy   unfit

The words should be the same as those already given, but with the prefix un– added to make them match the pictures. If the children write a word that matches the picture but does not begin with un– [e.g. sad; messy], ask them if they can think of another word beginning with un–, using the given word as a prompt.

40

Remember

Sometimes you add **un–** to a **doing word** (or **verb**).
It changes the word like this:

I tie my laces. Then I untie them.

More practice

1 Add **un–** to these **doing words** or **verbs**.

____un____ cover   ____un____ fold   ____un____ dress   ____un____ curl

____un____ roll   ____un____ bolt   ____un____ pick   ____un____ zip

2 Add **un–** to the **verb** in **bold**. Write each new **sentence**.

This key will **lock** the door.

This key will unlock the door.

I helped Jacob **pack** his bag.

I helped Jacob unpack his bag.

Max can **do** the zip on his jacket.

Max can undo the zip on his jacket.

The helpers will **load** the van.

The helpers will unload the van.

Check that the words beginning with un– are spelt correctly. They should be written as one word [i.e. with no space between un– and the verb].

New sentences should be correctly punctuated.

Sentence practice

Add **un–** to the **verb** below. Write a sentence using the new **word**.

block

I saw the woman unblock the drain.

41

This is just an example of a sentence using the verb 'unblock' in a suitable context.

Check that the sentence is correctly punctuated.

Revision 3 answers

Focus: using 'and' to join sentences [or clauses]

The children should use the word 'and' to join the two sentences together in one sentence.

Check that the sentences are correctly punctuated with no capital letter for 'and' or the word after it.

These pages revise ideas introduced in Sections 2 and 3. The focus of each activity is given to help identify areas where the children might need further revision.

Grammar 1   Schofield & Sims **Grammar and Punctuation**

Revision 3

1 Write the two sentences as <u>one</u> **sentence**.

We played snakes and ladders. I won.

We played snakes and ladders and I won.

Bella went to the park. She played on her bike.

Bella went to the park and she played on her bike.

2 Write the missing **punctuation mark** at the end of each speech bubble.

Focus: using sentence punctuation: full stops, question marks, exclamation marks

Reading the sentences aloud will help the children distinguish between them, particularly the difference between 'I can help you.' and 'Can I help you?' [Note: The children will learn more about this in **Grammar 2**.]

42

78

Schofield & Sims Grammar and Punctuation

Grammar 1

3 Underline the **words** that need a **capital letter**.

Then <u>hansel</u> and <u>gretel</u> got lost in the wood.

We went to <u>blackpool</u> last <u>saturday</u>.

Mum said <u>i</u> should tell <u>mr jackson</u>.

My school is on <u>blake street</u>

Focus: using capital letters for names, 'I' and days of the week

The first word of each sentence does not need to be underlined as it already has a capital letter.

4 You can add **un–** to <u>three</u> of these **words**. Underline the three words.

rude   <u>selfish</u>   <u>tidy</u>   soft   good   <u>kind</u>

Now write the three words with **un–**.

___unselfish___   ___untidy___   ___unkind___

Focus: using the prefix un– to change the meaning of adjectives

The words should be spelt correctly with no space after un–.

5 Add the correct **endings** to the **words** in **bold**.

Mrs Black is my **teach**_er____.

She is **teach**_ing____ us about plants and flowers.

Yesterday she **show**_ed____ us a sunflower.

Today we are **learn**_ing____ about seeds.

Focus: using verb endings

In the third sentence, 'she shows us a sunflower' makes sense but the word 'yesterday' tells us it should be 'showed'. [Note: The children will learn more about verb endings and past and present tense in **Grammar 2**.]

6 Rewrite each **sentence**, adding in <u>two</u> **describing words**.

The man sat on the bench.

The old man sat on the green bench.

The elephant spoke to the fly.

The big elephant spoke to the tiny fly.

The boy played with the kitten.

The happy boy played with the black kitten.

43

Focus: adding extra describing words to give detail

These are just examples. The children may have added different words. Discuss their choices.

Check that their sentences are correctly punctuated.

Writing task 3: Analysis sheet

Tick the circles to show amount of evidence found in writing:
1 No evidence
2 Some evidence
3 Clear evidence

Pupil name: _____

Date: _____

Assessing punctuation

The writing sample demonstrates:	Evidence		
capital letters used at the beginning of sentences.	①	②	③
sentence boundaries recognised and demarcated with full stops.	①	②	③
question marks and exclamation marks used appropriately [e.g. Have you been? It was great!].	①	②	③
capital letters used for 'I', names of people and places, days of the week and the months of the year.	①	②	③
capital letters used only where needed – no incorrect use [e.g. in the middle of words or sentences].	①	②	③

Assessing grammar and sentence structure

The writing sample demonstrates:	Evidence		
words formed into complete sentences.	①	②	③
grammatically correct sentences [e.g. no missing words; correct verb endings].	①	②	③
appropriate spacing between words.	①	②	③
the word 'and' used to join words and clauses [e.g. We went on a ride and it was fun.].	①	②	③
sentences sequenced using some simple linking words [e.g. Then ...; Next ...].	①	②	③
some added detail [e.g. using describing words or adjectives].	①	②	③

Key target: _____

Writing task 3: Pupil checklist

Name: _____   Date: _____

Reread what you have written to check that it makes sense. Tick the circle if you have correctly used the punctuation or grammar feature in your writing.

Punctuation

◯ I have used capital letters at the beginning of sentences.

◯ I have used full stops at the end of sentences.

◯ I have used a question mark or exclamation mark when one is needed.

◯ I have used capital letter 'I' for names, the days of the week and the months of the year.

Grammar and sentences

◯ I have said my sentences aloud before writing them.

◯ I have checked that my sentences make sense and are complete.

◯ I have left spaces between my words.

◯ I have used the word 'and' to join words and to make a longer sentence.

◯ I have used words like 'Then' and 'Next' to link sentences in order.

◯ I have used describing words to add extra detail.

Teacher feedback

My key target: _____

_____

_____

Final test

Name: _____

1 Write the words in order so that they make a **sentence**.

the play I garden. in

_____

1 mark

2 Add some **words** to make these words into a **sentence**. Write the sentence. Use the correct **punctuation**.

cold   today

_____

1 mark

3 Write in the missing **word** to complete the sentence.

The little boy ran _____ ran.

1 mark

4 Tick the <u>one</u> sentence that is correct.

I saw emma outside. ☐

I think i will go for a run. ☐

I saw Della skipping. ☐

I help harry read his book. ☐

1 mark

5 Tick the correct **word** to complete the sentence below.

The bell rings _____ the children come out to play.

Next ☐

Then ☐

and ☐

Later ☐

1 mark

6 Write the missing **punctuation mark** to complete the sentence.

How did you get here____

1 mark

7 Underline the **words** that need to start with a **capital letter**.

Dad took me to bristol on sunday.

1 mark

8 Write **–s** or **–es** to make each word a **plural**.

star_____

torch_____

flame_____

1 mark

9 Write a **word** to complete the sentence.

Sam has a _____ bag.

1 mark

10 Tick the correct **doing word** or (**verb**) to complete the sentence below.

Kate is _____ up and down.

jump ☐

jumps ☐

jumping ☐

jumped ☐

1 mark

11 Tick the <u>one</u> sentence that has the correct **punctuation**.

What is your name! ☐

that hurt! ☐

Go away! ☐

I will visit Susie ☐

☐ 1 mark

12 Tick the <u>two</u> words that you can add **un–** to.

_____shut ☐   _____lock ☐

_____slam ☐   _____bolt ☐

☐ 1 mark

13 Add the missing **full stop** and **capital letter**.

Polly was in the garden she was playing on her bike.

☐ 1 mark

14 Write the next sentence to say what happened. Start your sentence with a **linking word**.

First we had our breakfast. _____

_____

☐ 1 mark

End of test

Final test: Mark scheme

Q	Focus	Answer
1	combining words to make sentences	**Award 1 mark** for the correct sentence ending with a full stop. I play in the garden. Do not award a mark if the words are not clearly spaced.
2	writing a single sentence with a capital letter and full stop	**Award 1 mark** for an appropriate sentence with clear spacing that starts with a capital letter and ends with a full stop, e.g. It is cold today. I think it is cold today.
3	joining words using 'and'	**Award 1 mark** for the word 'and'. The little boy ran and ran.
4	using capital letters for names and 'I'	**Award 1 mark** for the correct box ticked. I saw Della skipping. ✓
5	joining clauses using 'and'	**Award 1 mark** for the correct box ticked. and ✓
6	using question marks to demarcate questions	**Award 1 mark** for correctly adding a question mark. How did you get here?
7	using capital letters for names of places and days of the week	**Award 1 mark** for <u>both</u> words correctly identified. Dad took me to <u>bristol</u> on <u>sunday</u>. *Do not accept* 'Dad' as one of the words as it already starts with a capital letter.
8	adding regular plural noun suffixes –s or –es	**Award 1 mark** for all <u>three</u> correct endings added. stars torches flames

Q	Focus	Answer
9	adding describing words in sentences	**Award 1 mark** for any suitable describing word, e.g. new, red/blue/green, nice, heavy
10	using verbs and verb endings	**Award 1 mark** for the correct box ticked. jumping ✓
11	using exclamation marks to demarcate sentences	**Award 1 mark** for the correct box ticked. Go away! ✓
12	using the prefix un– to change the meaning of verbs	**Award 1 mark** for the <u>two</u> words correctly identified. ____lock ✓ ____bolt ✓ Award the mark if pupils have written un– on the line instead.
13	demarcating sentence boundaries with capital letters and full stops	**Award 1 mark** for a capital letter and a full stop added in the correct position. Polly was in the garden. She was playing on her bike.
14	sequencing sentences to form short narratives	**Award 1 mark** for an appropriate sentence that starts with a linking word, e.g. Then we played outside. Next we went to brush our teeth.

Final test: Analysis sheet

Tick the box for each correct answer.

Q	Focus	Pupil names										
1	combining words to make sentences											
2	writing a single sentence with a capital letter and full stop											
3	joining words using 'and'											
4	using capital letters for names and 'I'											
5	joining clauses using 'and'											
6	using question marks to demarcate questions											
7	using capital letters for place names and days of the week											
8	adding regular plural noun suffixes –s or –es											
9	adding describing words in sentences											
10	using verbs and verb endings											
11	using exclamation marks to demarcate sentences											
12	using the prefix un– to change the meaning of verbs											
13	demarcating sentence boundaries with capital letters and full stops											
14	sequencing sentences											
Total correct answers per pupil												

Target tracking sheet

Group: _____

Target: _____

Date set: _____ Date for review: _____

Tick the circles to show depth of understanding:
1 Just beginning
2 Progressing
3 Learning is embedded

Pupil name	Evidence from independent writing	Progress in independent writing
		① ② ③
		① ② ③
		① ② ③
		① ② ③
		① ② ③
		① ② ③
		① ② ③
		① ② ③
		① ② ③
		① ② ③

Learning pathways sheet

Pupil name: _____

Date last updated: _____

Tick the circles to show depth of understanding:
1 Just beginning
2 Progressing
3 Learning is embedded

Punctuation pathway

Demarcate a single sentence with a capital letter and full stop.

① ② ③

Use capital letters for the names of people and 'I'.

① ② ③

Use capital letters for the names of people, places, 'I' and the days of the week.

① ② ③

Use a question mark at the end of a question.

① ② ③

Use an exclamation mark where appropriate.

① ② ③

Demarcate at least three sentences with capital letters and full stops [or '?' or '!'].

① ② ③

Grammar and sentence pathway

Say and write a single complete sentence.

① ② ③

Write a sentence leaving spaces between words.

① ② ③

Say and write ideas in complete sentences.

① ② ③

Use 'and' to join words or clauses in a sentence.

① ② ③

Write a sequence of sentences using words such as 'then' and 'next'.

① ② ③

Use some simple describing words to add detail.

① ② ③

Glossary

Adjective

An **adjective** is a word used to modify or specify a noun [e.g. an <u>angry</u> man; the <u>red</u> car].
Many simple adjectives *describe* the noun so in Grammar 1 adjectives are called 'describing words'.
Lesson 14

- Some adjectives are formed by adding a suffix to a word [e.g. care<u>ful</u>; care<u>less</u>]. Grammar 2
- The suffixes –er and –est are used to form **comparative adjectives** [e.g. smaller] and **superlative adjectives** [e.g. smallest]. These adjectives are used when comparing nouns. Grammar 2

Adverb

An **adverb** is a word that modifies a verb or action, for example, saying *how* the action is performed [e.g. He sat <u>quietly</u>. The ship sailed <u>smoothly</u>.]. Grammar 2

Many adverbs are formed by adding the suffix –ly to an adjective [e.g. kind<u>ly</u>]. However, not all adverbs end with –ly [e.g. She stood <u>still</u>. She ran <u>fast</u>.]. Grammar 2

Apostrophe

An **apostrophe [']** is a punctuation mark used:

- to show missing letters in **shortened forms** [contractions] [e.g. can't]. Grammar 2
- to show **possession** [e.g. Sam's hat]. Grammar 2

Comma

A **comma [,]** is a punctuation mark used within sentences [e.g. to separate items in a list]. Grammar 2

Conjunction

A **conjunction** is a word that joins two words or clauses together [e.g. and, but; because, when]. In Grammar 1 and Grammar 2 the phrase 'joining word' is used in place of 'conjunction'. Lessons 5 and 6

There are two types of conjunction, although pupils do not need to know this terminology in Key Stage 1:

- **co-ordinating conjunctions** [and, but, or]. Lessons 5 and 6, Grammar 2
- **subordinating conjunctions** [e.g. because; when; if]. Grammar 2

Noun

Nouns are words that name things, places, people [e.g. car; park; man]. These are **common nouns**.
Grammar 2

- **Proper nouns** are the names of specific people, places or things [e.g. Joe; Banbury Park; July]. Proper nouns start with a capital letter. Lessons 3 and 7
- A **compound noun** is a noun made up of two root words joined together [e.g. footpath]. Grammar 2
- A **noun phrase** is a group of words that expand on a noun [e.g. car → the fast police car]. The other words added to the noun 'car' tell us more about it. Grammar 2

Prefixes and suffixes

A **prefix** is added to the start of a word to make it into another word [e.g. <u>un</u>do]. Lesson 15
A **suffix** is added to the end of a word to change how we use the word [e.g. forming adjectives – peace<u>ful</u>, harm<u>less</u>; or nouns – amaze<u>ment</u>]. Grammar 2

Sentence

A **sentence** is a group of words connected together that makes sense/says something. A sentence starts with a capital letter and ends with a full stop [or '?' or '!']. Lessons 1, 2, 4 and 12

There are different forms of sentence with different functions and different grammatical patterns:

- **Questions** ask for information or need a response. They begin with a question word or a subject–verb reversal, and end with question mark [e.g. <u>What</u> is the weather like today? <u>Is it</u> cold today?]. Lesson 9
- **Statements** give information. They usually start with subject–verb [e.g. <u>Joe ran</u> away. <u>It is</u> cold today.]. Grammar 2
- **Exclamations** express strong emotion and end with an exclamation mark. A strict definition of an exclamation refers to sentences starting with 'What' or 'How' [e.g. What a surprise! How amazing!]. However, interjections are also exclamatory [e.g. Oh dear!]. Grammar 2
- **Commands** direct someone to do something. The main clause often starts with a verb [e.g. Come here.]. Grammar 2

We sometimes add exclamation marks to statements or commands to make exclamatory statements or exclamatory commands [e.g. It was great! Help!]. However, this does not change the form of the sentence.

Sentence punctuation

Sentence punctuation refers to the use of capital letters, full stops, question marks and exclamation marks to show the boundaries between sentences.

- **Capital letters** are used to mark the beginning of a sentence. They are also used at the start of names and for the word 'I'. Lessons 2, 3, 7 and 12
- A **full stop** is used to mark the end of a sentence. Lesson 2
- A **question mark [?]** is used in place of a full stop if a sentence is a question. Lesson 9
- An **exclamation mark [!]** is used if the sentence is an exclamation or to show strong feeling. Lesson 11

Singular and plural

Many nouns have singular and plural forms. **Singular** means there is just one of something; **plural** means there is more than one of something. Plural forms are usually formed by adding –s or –es to the noun [e.g. cat<u>s</u>; dog<u>s</u>; fox<u>es</u>]. Lesson 8

Verb

A verb is a 'doing' or 'being' word [e.g. He <u>ran</u>. He <u>is</u> sad.]. Verbs are important because they tell us about the actions in a sentence. Lesson 10

- Verbs in a sentence usually have a **tense**. The tense of a verb tells us *when* the action happened – in the **past** or the **present**. Many simple **past tense verbs** are formed by adding –ed [e.g. jumped; stopped]. Other verbs have irregular **past tense** forms [e.g. have/had; see/saw]. Grammar 2
- **Progressive forms** [also called 'continuous'] can be used in the present and past tense to describe events in progress, or events that were in progress, for some time. They use the –ing form of the verb with the helper verb is/are/am or was/were [e.g. he <u>is</u> sing<u>ing</u>; she <u>was</u> walk<u>ing</u>]. Grammar 2